Unlocking the Success Puzzle

Ten Practical Rules to Achieve Your Goals

Andres Kuusk

Previous Books

Financial contagion: a meta-analysis based approach (978-3659557194), LAP LAMBERT Academic Publishing, 2014

Unlocking the Success Puzzle

Ten Practical Rules to Achieve Your Goals

Andres Kuusk

BUSINESS BOOKS
London, UK
Washington, DC, USA

CollectiveInk

First published by Business Books, 2026
Business Books is an imprint of Collective Ink Ltd.,
Unit 11, Shepperton House, 89 Shepperton Road, London, N1 3DF
office@collectiveink.com
www.collectiveink.com
www.collectiveink.com/business-books

For distributor details and how to order please visit the 'Ordering' section on our website.

ISBN: 978 1 78535 650 6
978 1 78535 998 9 (ebook)
Library of Congress Control Number: 2025930407

A CIP catalogue record for this book is available from the British Library.

Design: Lapiz Digital Services

UK: Printed and bound by CPI Group (UK) Ltd, Croydon, CR0 4YY
Printed in North America by CPI GPS partners

The manufacturer's authorised representative in the EU for product safety is: eucomply OÜ - Pärnu mnt 139b-14, 11317 Tallinn, Estonia, hello@ eucompliancepartner.com, www.eucompliancepartner.com

We operate a distinctive and ethical publishing philosophy in all areas of our business, from our global network of authors to production and worldwide distribution.

Life is not a game of chance, it's a game of choice.

— Author

Contents

Acknowledgements

No book is written in isolation, and this one is no exception. It has been a journey of growth, challenge, and learning — and I owe my deepest gratitude to the many people who played a part in it.

First, to Katija, thank you for your patience, unwavering belief in me, and support throughout this process. Your calm encouragement kept me going, even when the pieces of this puzzle felt like they would never fit.

To my publishing team, Brian Mountford, Denise Smith, Frank Smecker, G.L. Davies, Nick Welch, Steve Wagstaff and Vicky Hartley; thank you for your sharp eye, thoughtful guidance, and relentless pursuit of clarity. Your expertise shaped this book into something far greater than I could have achieved alone.

To the many thinkers, strategists, and authors whose ideas influenced me — too numerous to name — thank you for challenging me to think bigger and deeper.

Finally, to you — the reader. This book exists for you. I hope it serves as a guide, a spark, or a lifeline on your journey toward success. Thank you for trusting me to walk alongside you on this path.

To everyone who played a role, large or small, thank you for being a part of this journey. This book exists because of you.

— Andres Kuusk

Introduction

The road to success is dotted with many tempting parking spaces.

Will Rogers

Stuck in a Parking Space

I was 25 when it hit me: I had comfortably parked in one of those tempting parking spaces. I wasn't on the road to success — I was stalled. My potential was rusting. Time was leaking away. I had no major achievements, no money, no love story, and no clue where I was headed.

But how had I ended up here?

When I got accepted into the most prestigious university in the country, I believed I was destined for greatness. Only a handful of people in my circle of friends and family had ever made it to a top-tier university, and I felt like I'd been given a head start. It seemed like a launchpad for success — the perfect foundation for an extraordinary life.

On top of that, I had my passion for mind sports and board games, which I believed would sharpen my thinking and fuel my personal growth. With these two pillars — education and passion — I convinced myself that success was inevitable.

For several years, I believed I was on the right track. My days were packed with activities that felt productive and meaningful. I attended lectures with genuine enthusiasm, soaking up knowledge like a sponge. Evenings were filled with friendly board games, sports matches, and movie nights with friends. Weekends were dedicated to chess tournaments and family visits. My life was busy, colorful, and filled with just enough moments that *felt* like success to keep me convinced I was moving forward. I had no reason to question it. I was too entertained to notice.

Then something changed.

The Moment of Truth

One day, it hit me like a spotlight I didn't even know I was standing under. For the first time, I saw my life from a distance, and I didn't like what I saw. It wasn't one of those "gradual realizations" you hear about. It was a sharp, unfiltered, and uncomfortable truth crashing down on me. Perhaps it was the slow erosion of my self-deception, or maybe I'd just run out of distractions to keep me blind.

But the facade of "progress" crumbled. I wanted something real. Something meaningful. I realized I'd been living in denial, keeping myself busy with activities that looked like growth but weren't.

Although I had some skill in mind sports, I had never truly excelled. I had never won a national championship, not even in a youth or junior category. My academic path seemed promising — after all, I was studying at a top university — but I had no plan for what to do after graduation. My social life was equally hollow. Outside of my studies and mind sports, I had no identity. I was the stereotypical unsociable nerd who dodged parties and avoided public speaking like it was a contagious disease. My social circle consisted exclusively of board game enthusiasts. I had no job, no car, and no long-term relationship to speak of.

Speaking of relationships, I had a hopeless crush on a university classmate, Birgit. In my mind, we were destined to be a power couple — the kind of dynamic duo people would write books about. In reality, Birgit barely knew I existed. I thought it was love, but in hindsight, it feels more like "borderline stalking with academic justification." I only feel comfortable confessing it now because, fortunately, the statute of limitations has expired.

In short, I was living a life with no notable achievements, no romance, no sustainable income, and no clear plan for the future. I told myself this was acceptable, but deep down, I knew it wasn't. I knew I was lying to myself.

And when I finally confronted that lie, everything changed.

At that moment of self-reflection, I saw my life for what it truly was — wasted potential, days turning into weeks, weeks into years. I didn't want to waste any more of it. I promised myself I would finally chase the goals I had quietly carried in my mind for years but had never dared to pursue. I wanted to succeed. I wanted to break free from the person I had been.

But I knew I couldn't do that with the same mindset I'd always had. I needed a radical shift — not just a minor tweak or an upgrade. I needed a complete overhaul. I needed to become something more.

I needed to become Andres 2.0.

Becoming Andres 2.0

It's not enough to be talented. It's not enough to work hard or study late into the night. You must also become intimately aware of the methods you use to reach your decisions.

Garry Kasparov

I became a philosopher of my own life, analyzing every aspect of it and searching for the path to tangible success. At first, I believed success was a simple formula: luck plus hard work equals success. But that belief didn't last long. No matter how relentlessly I worked, success didn't always follow. Sometimes, despite my best efforts, I fell short. Other times, success came so easily it felt like I had cheated.

It became clear that talent, hard work, and luck weren't the whole story. There was something else at play — something hidden beneath the surface. I didn't know it yet, but that "something else" would change the way I saw everything.

I had to find that "something else."

I decided to approach my life like a grand experiment, with myself as both the scientist and the subject. Every decision became a kind of A/B test. I tested different strategies, routines, and ideas — some inspired by books, others born from my own intuition. Sure, the sample size of my personal experiences wasn't large enough for scientists to draw conclusions from, but I had no better option than to attribute my wins to good decisions and my failures to bad ones.

Over time, I began to see patterns. Certain strategies worked like magic, while others felt like blind shots in the dark. The more I experimented, the more I realized that success wasn't a straight line — it was a puzzle.

To solve a jigsaw puzzle, you don't need to see the entire picture right away. You start with a few connected pieces, and little by little, the image takes shape. Success was no different. Each new concept I learned felt like one of those puzzle pieces locking into place. I didn't need to see the whole picture to know I was making progress — I could feel it. The more pieces I connected, the clearer everything became. The more parts of the puzzle I put together, the higher my odds of success became, even if I didn't have all the answers.

Piece by piece, I assembled the puzzle of success. Each new discovery revealed the crucial differences between success and failure. Over time, I reached a level of efficiency I never thought possible. While others toiled and struggled, I was achieving the same results with a fraction of the effort.

And then something unexpected happened. Some of these puzzle pieces didn't just "fit" — they reinforced one another. The pieces had a synergistic effect, amplifying each other's impact. It was like putting together a puzzle and suddenly realizing that two pieces, when combined, create something bigger than the sum of their parts.

I learned that it wasn't about how hard I worked but how smart I worked. It wasn't about quantity, but quality. It wasn't about talent, luck, or even raw perseverance. It was about strategy.

By the end of it, I had done it. I had achieved my goal.

I had become Andres 2.0.

How Everything Changed

A decade after that pivotal moment, I was no longer the same person. From no national championship titles, I had moved up to forty. I wasn't just a national champion — I had achieved the prestigious title of World Champion in Mind Sports, also known as The Pentamind. And not just once, but four times (eventually adding two more titles to my tally).

Beyond mind sports, I also pursued academic success, earning both a master's and a PhD in Economics. This academic journey opened doors to a rewarding career where I held positions as a professor of Game Theory at a prestigious university and later as a top Risk Manager at successful tech companies.

On a personal level, the transformation was just as profound. I had a girlfriend who turned heads wherever she went — yet she chose me (while Birgit, as fate would have it, still had no idea I existed). Financially, I achieved freedom through passive income that covered all my expenses. And to top it off, I finally bought my own car. Yes, it was "just" a Škoda, but it had four wheels, an engine, and it got me where I needed to go — so I counted it as a win.

Not bad for a guy who, for 25 years, had failed to achieve anything of real significance.

How did this transformation happen? How did someone who had been "average at best" for most of his life suddenly crack the code to success and turn nearly everything he touched into gold?

This wasn't a Cinderella story where success magically found me by chance. It wasn't untapped "natural talent" suddenly surfacing after years of dormancy. Every victory required deliberate effort and learning — sometimes painfully slow, sometimes brutally frustrating. There was no luxury in my journey — no fairy godmother, no magic wand, no secret shortcut to glory. I had to walk the hard road, step by step.

But in hindsight, that was a gift, not a burden.

The slow, deliberate learning process gave me the chance to do something most people never do: figure out the system behind success. I had the opportunity to analyze each failure, each small victory, and every pattern I encountered along the way. Piece by piece, I outlined the key components of what I now call the success puzzle.

What This Book Will Do for You

And that's what this book is here to do — to give you the pieces of the puzzle that I spent 10 years piecing together.

I'm not claiming to have discovered every secret to success. I'm not claiming to have unlocked the "ultimate success formula." But I have gathered plenty of effective insights, tips, and strategies that worked for me and for others I've studied. In this book, I present them as rules — ingredients in the success formula — that act as stepping stones toward your desired outcomes.

My definition of success is simple: success is achieving the goals you set for yourself.

This definition works because success is relative. Different people have different goals, and that's perfectly fine. Others may try to convince you to chase *their* definition of success, but true success is defined by whether you achieve *your own* goals. If your goal is to build a business, success is building that business. If your goal is to master chess, success is mastering chess. And if you believe that happiness is the only thing that matters in life, then that is your goal — and achieving it is your success.

This book is about helping you reach *your* success — not mine, not anyone else's. Yours.

The main focus of the book is to unlock the potential for success that exists in all of us, so that we can achieve more with less effort. I know that might sound too good to be true, but it's entirely possible — if you learn to avoid the most common pitfalls that hinder progress. And these pitfalls deserve a closer look.

The Hidden Traps Holding You Back

It's easier to fool people than to convince them that they have been fooled.

Mark Twain

Despite what we like to believe, humans aren't as rational or in control of their actions as we think. Just like every other species on Earth, our behavior is shaped by evolution. On the bright side, evolution has given us flexible brains and an innate curiosity to learn and grow. This gives us the potential to achieve almost any realistic goal we set for ourselves. Our capacity for learning, adaptation, and self-improvement is unmatched in the animal kingdom.

But evolution didn't just hand us the "good stuff." It also left us with a few "features" we didn't ask for. Chief among them is the tendency to conserve energy. From an evolutionary standpoint, this made perfect sense. Back when food was scarce and predators were plentiful, wasting energy could get you killed. If you burned too many calories chasing a rabbit just for fun, you might not have the energy to outrun a lion later that day. So, evolution hardwired us to avoid unnecessary effort.

The problem? We're no longer dodging lions or scrounging for berries. But that same instinct to "conserve energy" is still with us, silently influencing our decisions. It's why we scroll on our phones, ignore uncomfortable issues, give up early, or convince ourselves that a task is harder than it really is. Our brains aren't lazy — they're efficient. But that efficiency becomes a liability when it talks us out of pursuing something worthwhile. It's one of the core concepts behind several of the rules in this book: when it comes to achieving your goals, your natural instincts are often your biggest obstacle. Nobody can sabotage your goals quite like you can. Your brain, thinking it's "protecting" you, convinces you to avoid action or quit far too soon.

If we could resist the urge to hold back or give up entirely, we'd unlock our full potential. We'd tap into the power to persevere, learn, and grow far beyond what most of us think is possible. The problem is you can't completely override your evolutionary programming. Changing human nature is one of the hardest feats imaginable (and no book or rule can eliminate laziness entirely). As Mark Twain astutely observed, "It's easier to fool people than to convince them that they have been fooled." And when it comes to laziness, it's our evolutionary biology doing the fooling. Fortunately, while you can't "fix" human nature, you can trick yourself into acting as though you have.

That's where this book comes in.

The rules you'll learn here aren't about "fixing" your nature. They're designed to outsmart it. These rules aren't about brute-forcing your way to success — they're about quietly sidestepping your natural instincts to conserve energy, turn a blind eye to personal challenges, or quit prematurely. Each rule invites you to take one small, simple action — but beneath that action, something far more profound is happening. In essence, these rules trick you into behaving as though you've already conquered your instincts — even if you haven't. (Your brain will still think you're as lazy as you were before reading this book, but you'll act as if you weren't.)

That's why this book works.

How This Book Will Change Your Game

The goal of this book is simple: to help you achieve more while doing less. To do that, it introduces clever, practical rules designed to outsmart your brain's natural instincts. These rules are simple to understand and easy to apply — but don't mistake simplicity for weakness. Their impact on your ability to achieve your goals is profound.

To ensure each rule is both practical and powerful, I set five key criteria that every rule had to meet:

- **Clarity**: If a 12-year-old can't understand it, it's not clear enough.
- **Practicality**: If you can't use it frequently, it's not practical.
- **Ease of Use**: If it's too complex or time-consuming, you won't do it.
- **Problem-Solving Orientation**: Every rule tackles common problems with high harm potential.
- **Systematic Fit**: Each rule strengthens the system, with every rule reinforcing the others.

Each rule in this book primarily addresses one specific problem that hinders people from achieving their goals, though some rules tackle multiple challenges. These problems are rooted in common human tendencies — laziness, self-doubt, blind spots, and more. By identifying these problems, I was able to reverse-engineer practical solutions. Each chapter targets a specific challenge and presents a simple, memorable rule to overcome it.

Common Problems and the Chapters That Solve Them

- Choosing the wrong goals — Chapter 1
- Giving up too soon — Chapters 2, 5, and 6
- Being inefficient with your time and effort — Chapter 3
- Failing to take control when it matters most — Chapter 4
- Getting frustrated and losing motivation because of small failures — Chapter 5
- Underestimating your chances of success — Chapter 6
- Making impulsive, emotion-driven decisions — Chapter 7

- Failing to realize what truly matters — Chapters 7 and 8
- Cutting yourself off from success potential — Chapter 8
- Ignoring your personal flaws and critical issues in your life — Chapter 9
- Being unambitious and settling for mediocrity — Chapters 2, 4, and 10

The 10-Step Roadmap to Success

This book is divided into ten chapters, with each chapter dedicated to one specific rule. Every rule begins with a real-world story (often from my own life) so you can see the problem in action. As the story unfolds, you'll begin to sense the logical need for a specific rule. By the time the rule is formally introduced, it will already feel familiar and relevant. This approach ensures you not only understand the rule but also recognize how and why it works.

The chapters are arranged in a logical sequence. The first five chapters follow the natural lifecycle of goal achievement — from choosing which goals to pursue to handling the disappointment of setbacks. The figure below illustrates this journey:

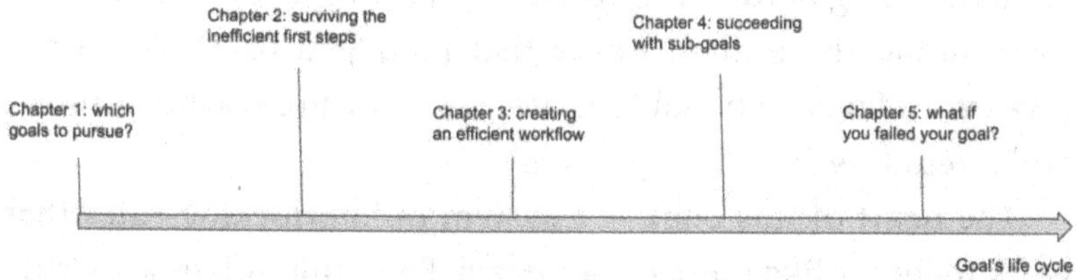

Here's the flow of the first five chapters:

- **Chapter 1**: Choose the right goals to pursue.
- **Chapter 2**: Tackle early obstacles and avoid premature disappointment
- **Chapter 3**: Streamline your workflow for maximum efficiency.

- **Chapter 4**: Achieve critical short-term event-related goals.
- **Chapter 5**: Overcome setbacks and stay emotionally resilient

The next three chapters (Chapters 6, 7, and 8) focus on career-related goals, which make up a large part of our ambitions. These chapters offer rules for navigating the unique challenges of work and career progression.

Finally, the last two chapters (Chapters 9 and 10) take a broader approach, addressing personal growth and life success. They contain strategies for mastering your inner world and your interactions with others. By the end of the tenth chapter, you will have assembled ten critical pieces of the success puzzle.

But don't stop there. The final summary reveals how these pieces fit together to form a unified, powerful system. It's not just a collection of isolated rules — it's a complete blueprint for success.

Why This Book Is a Game-Changer

Most self-help books tell you to "work harder" or "believe in yourself" — but this book takes a vastly different path. It's not about hustling harder. It's about outsmarting your instincts and overcoming the hidden forces that hold you back. This book gives you clever, actionable strategies to do more, achieve more, and stress less.

The heart of this book is a system of interlocking rules that work together like pieces of a puzzle. Each rule solves a specific problem that prevents people from achieving their goals. As the puzzle comes together, you'll see how every small win strengthens the next, creating a compounding effect on your success.

These rules help you avoid the traps that most people don't even realize they're falling into. By mastering them, you'll have a serious advantage over those who don't know them.

If you've ever felt like success is reserved for "gifted" people with "special talents," this book will shatter that illusion. There is no "success gene" and no secret club for "naturally gifted" people. If you've ever felt like you were missing some "magic secret" that successful people knew but you didn't — this book will give you that secret.

Success isn't magic. It's a puzzle made of pieces you can control.

Here's what you'll gain from this book:

- **Clarity**: Know exactly which goals to pursue and which to drop.
- **Efficiency**: Get more done in less time, with less effort.
- **Mental Resilience**: Bounce back from failure and stay on track.
- **Decision-Making Skills**: Make smarter, faster decisions.
- **Objectivity**: Stop fooling yourself and start seeing reality as it is.
- **A Success System**: Master a complete, unified system — not random tips or tricks.

I truly believe this book can be a guiding light on your journey to success. Looking back, I can't help but wonder how much faster I could have achieved my goals if I'd had this book at 25. I spent years piecing together the success puzzle, but you can do it much faster. With this book as your guide, you have the advantage I never had.

You're at the starting line, with the first puzzle piece already in your hand.

All you have to do is turn the page.

Chapter 1

Every Master Was Once a Beginner

The journey of a thousand miles begins with one step.
Lao Tzu

The Parable of the Carpenter

A seasoned carpenter was ready to retire after years of dedicated work. Before he could hang up his tools, his employer made a special request — to build one last house. Reluctantly, the carpenter agreed to take on the task, but as he worked on the construction, his lack of enthusiasm was palpable. His usual dedication and precision were nowhere to be found, as evidenced by the subpar materials and sloppy workmanship he used.

When the house was finished, the employer surprised him: "This house is my gift to you." The carpenter was stunned. Had he known he was building his future home, he would have poured his heart into it rather than rushing to get it done.

***

The Quoridor Experiment

There's a first time for everything — even for world-class champions. Michael Jordan once played his first basketball game, Bill Gates wrote his first computer program, and J.K. Rowling penned her first book. One thing they all have in common? Their first attempts weren't exactly masterpieces.

First attempts rarely lead to greatness — after all, you're still inexperienced. So when I sat down to play my first game of Quoridor, I wasn't expecting a Hollywood-style victory. But I had one thing working in my favor: I was hungry to improve.

That hunger, I hoped, would make up for my lack of experience. Spoiler alert — it didn't.

To understand how it all went down, we need to jump back to the early 2010s. Picture me in my small but cozy apartment, hunched over a Quoridor rulebook, eyes locked in as if it held the secrets of the universe. This wasn't just any casual game night — Quoridor was part of the Pentamind World Championships schedule, and I was determined to master it.

Once I had the rules down, I went online to find an opponent. I didn't care who it was — I just needed an opponent. I found a platform and spotted a player looking for a game. His profile made it clear he wasn't a rookie, but I wasn't intimidated.

Pause here for a moment, dear reader. Here's your chance to make a prediction. I'm a complete novice, facing off against an experienced player, but I had something on my side: motivation and laser-sharp focus. Do you think I won my very first game, or did I face defeat? Take a second to lock in your answer.

If you believed in me and guessed "victory" — I admire your optimism. But, you should have known better — after all, this was my very first game and my opponent was an experienced player. Plus you were given a spoiler alert. I didn't just lose — I got *obliterated*. It wasn't even close. It was like bringing a toothpick to a sword fight.

For most people, that first loss would have been the end of their Quoridor journey. They'd log off, blame the game, blame the opponent's "luck," or convince themselves that Quoridor "just isn't for them." It's the classic tale of the fox and the sour grapes — if you can't have the grapes, convince yourself you never wanted them in the first place.

But that's not my style.

Instead of walking away, I rewatched the entire game. Move by move, I studied it like it was game footage before the playoffs. What did my opponent do that I didn't see? What moves had

I missed? Where did I go wrong? I took notes, analyzed the patterns, and challenged him to a rematch.

With one game of experience under my belt, I was sure I'd fare better. Did I win the second game? Nope. I lost – and I lost badly.

But did I give up? Absolutely not.

This time, I rewatched *both* games, comparing them to spot recurring mistakes. I started to see patterns. I started to see strategies behind my opponent's moves.

Armed with this new insight, I challenged him to a third game.

Let's play the prediction game again.

Do you think I finally won game three, or did I lose again? Lock in your answer.

If you guessed "victory," you clearly have faith in me. And I can tell you that this time, something was different. The game was closer. The gap was shrinking. My moves weren't as weak as they used to be. It felt like progress.

But I lost again. And I still didn't have much of a chance.

I could have stopped there. Three losses in a row is a pretty clear signal that most people would take as a sign to quit. But to me, those three games weren't failures – they were free lessons. Each game revealed something new. Each loss was like a piece of a larger puzzle that I was slowly piecing together.

So I challenged him again.

And again.

And again.

By the end of the night, I had played ten straight games against the same opponent. Ten. Each one punctuated by a review session where I rewatched every move, every mistake, and every missed opportunity. My goal was to squeeze every ounce of learning from every single loss.

Now, dear reader, for the final time, make your prediction.

After nine straight defeats, did I finally win game ten, or did I lose for the tenth time in a row?

If you're thinking, *"Surely, after all that effort, he must have won game ten,"* I appreciate your faith. But, alas, reality had other plans. I lost. Again. Sorry to disappoint you.

The Secret to "Zero to Hero"

At this point, you might be thinking, *"This guy must be the worst Quoridor player in human history."* And honestly, I wouldn't blame you for that conclusion. Ten straight losses don't exactly paint the picture of a prodigy.

But here's the twist.

Just three years later, I won a gold medal at the Mind Sports Olympiad Quoridor tournament. And then, I did it again. And again. Three gold medals in total.

So, how did I go from being completely hopeless to becoming one of the best players in the world?

To answer that, we have to tackle a bigger question: Why are top-mind sports players so good at what they do?

When faced with this question, many people assume that elite players must have exceptional intelligence, extraordinary talent, or even supernatural abilities — or maybe some combination of all three. But if my Quoridor journey teaches us anything, it's that I don't fit into any of those categories. Despite having 10 chances to learn from my mistakes, I didn't have the "intelligence" to win even *one* game. Losing all 10 games in a row isn't exactly a glowing endorsement for "natural talent" either. And as for supernatural powers? If I had any, I would have used them by game two.

If it's not intelligence, talent, or superpowers, then what is it?

Here's the simple truth: Top-mind sports players are good at their games because they *play a lot of them.* There's no magic formula, no divine gift, and no "chosen one" prophecy. They just put in the effort — hours of practice, strategy, and study.

This may sound obvious, but it's a truth that many people refuse to accept when it comes to intellectual pursuits. Everyone agrees that Roger Federer wasn't born holding a tennis racket and that Tiger Woods didn't become a champion without thousands of hours on the golf course. But when it comes to chess, poker, or other mind sports, people are quick to attribute success to "genius" or "natural talent."

It's not true.

Just like Federer trained his way to greatness, so did Garry Kasparov. And just like them, I had to train, too. The same principle applies to every field. Nobody is born a master because every master was once a beginner.

The Conclusion of the Quoridor Experiment

Let's return to my Quoridor story and explore *why* I eventually succeeded. By now, you've probably figured out that it wasn't about talent, intelligence, or superhuman abilities. So what was it?

It was hard work, perseverance, and sheer resilience. These three qualities drove me forward. But here's the catch — simply "working hard" and "never giving up" isn't enough. While those principles sound noble, they're not practical or specific. I've worked hard and failed. I've persevered and still fallen short. Hard work alone doesn't guarantee success.

Here's a story to illustrate that point.

At one point, I decided to learn the programming language C#. It wasn't even my idea; it came from my boss, who casually suggested it. For some reason, I took it as a personal challenge, even though C# wasn't directly relevant to my role. I dove in, watched Pluralsight courses, read programming books, and committed to learning it. For weeks, I tried to "grind" my way to mastery.

But it didn't work.

Despite all that effort, I wasn't making meaningful progress. I felt stuck, uninspired, and on the verge of giving up. After a few weeks, I quit entirely. No medal for me this time.

So, here's the big question: Why was I willing to endure loss after loss with Quoridor, but I gave up on C# after just a few weeks? If perseverance is the key to success, shouldn't I have pushed through with C# too? Why didn't hard work, perseverance and sheer resilience work this time?

Here's the truth: Not all goals are worth pursuing. And not all effort is equal. Sometimes, you have to know when to walk away. But how do you know which goals to chase and which to let go of? How do you tell the difference between a challenge worth fighting for and a battle that's just a waste of energy?

That's where the hidden key to success comes in.

The Hidden Key to Success

Looking back, the answer seems glaringly obvious. It's almost embarrassing that it took me years to figure it out.

For a long time, I believed success was all about efficiency. Work efficiently, and you'll succeed. Work inefficiently, and you'll fail. Simple, right? Except it's not. The idea isn't *wrong*, but it's too vague to be useful. Efficiency doesn't explain why the same amount of effort sometimes produces spectacular results and other times leaves you spinning your wheels.

For years, I thought this difference was out of my control. But then, one day, I found the answer.

It happened in London, during a presentation by Francisco "Paco" de la Banda, a Spanish mind sports coach and former world champion. His lecture was about how to cultivate creativity in children, but what I learned that day went way beyond child development. Paco answered a question that had been nagging me for years: Why does hard work sometimes lead to breakthrough results, and other times feel like a colossal waste of energy?

His answer was simple, elegant, and unforgettable: curiosity.

As soon as Paco said it, I had my "Eureka" moment. *This is it.* True mastery doesn't come from hard work alone. It comes from curiosity-driven hard work. Curiosity is the engine of achievement.

You've probably heard the quote from Mark Twain:

"Make a living by doing what you enjoy, and you never have to work a day in your life."

That quote doesn't mean that you literally don't have to work; it means that when you're deeply curious about something, the work doesn't feel like a burden. It feels like a natural extension of your interests. You're pulled toward it instead of pushing yourself through it.

This perfectly explains why I thrived in Quoridor but quit C#. In Quoridor, I wasn't driven by the need to "grind" or "push through." I was driven by curiosity. I was obsessed with figuring out winning strategies. Every mistake revealed something new. Every analysis session felt like an adventure, not a chore.

> *Curiosity is the engine of achievement.*
>
> **Ken Robinson**

Why C# Failed (and Why Your Goals Might Fail Too)

Compare that to C#. There was no spark of curiosity. There was no inner drive to figure it out. It was a task I had adopted for no good reason. My only motivation was to satisfy someone else's suggestion, not my own curiosity.

Without curiosity, my efforts become half-hearted, and my progress slowed to a crawl. I found myself lacking the drive to truly explore the subject. My motivation waned, making it difficult to focus and absorb the information. As a result, I eventually gave up on the project and forgot everything I had learned from the experience. The lack of curiosity led to a total failure in achieving my goal.

I'm sure you've been in a similar situation. Someone suggests you do something – maybe it's framed as a "good idea" or something that "might help your future." On the surface, it sounds reasonable. But deep down, you know you're not interested. You give it a shot anyway, but your heart's not in it. The result? You either quit quickly or slog through it, resenting every second of the process.

Here are some classic examples:

- Your parents want you to study law, but you're more interested in psychology.
- You impulsively declare a New Year's resolution to learn piano, even though you've never had the slightest interest in musical instruments.
- A friend convinces you to join her for a 6 am jogging routine, even though you're not a morning person and you hate running.

At first, you push through it with sheer willpower. Maybe you stick with it for a few days or even a couple of weeks. But eventually, your energy runs dry. Studying law feels like a prison sentence when your heart is set on psychology. Piano practice feels more like punishment than passion. And waking up at 5:30 am to run? Let's be real – you're NOT a morning person and you HATE running. What good could possibly come out of that?

Without curiosity, it's nearly impossible to put in your best effort. You'll quit, and worse, you'll blame yourself for quitting. That's why the first rule of the success formula is this:

The Rule of Curiosity:

Follow your curiosity. Focus your efforts on activities that genuinely interest you and eliminate the ones that don't.

Why does this work? When you pursue something you're not curious about, motivation dwindles. This leads to half-hearted efforts and an inability to dedicate the time and energy required for success. On the other hand, curiosity acts as a natural fuel for learning, focus, and perseverance. It creates the perfect conditions for giving your best effort and achieving peak efficiency.

> *For artists, scientists, inventors, schoolchildren, and the rest of us, intrinsic motivation – the drive to do something because it is interesting, challenging, and absorbing – is essential for high levels of creativity.*
>
> **Daniel H. Pink**

Curiosity is an intrinsic drive to learn. It's why learning something you're deeply curious about doesn't feel like "work" at all. Instead, it feels like play. When you're curious, work becomes enjoyable, not burdensome. It's as if the hours melt away, and the learning process becomes its own reward. This is why curiosity is a game-changer. It triggers a mental state where effort feels effortless, making it possible to work harder, longer, and more efficiently than you ever thought possible — without burning out.

Addressing a Common Misconception

There's a popular idiom you've probably heard: "Curiosity killed the cat." For decades, it's been used as a warning against being too curious. But here's something you might not know: that's only half the phrase. The full idiom actually goes, "Curiosity killed the cat, but satisfaction brought it back."

I'd argue that curiosity has done far more good than harm — and I even have my own spin on the phrase: "Curiosity killed the cat ... but saved the catkind."

Without curiosity, cats (and people) would remain stuck in survival mode – never exploring, never innovating, never growing. Curious people may seem annoying at times, constantly asking "Why?" and "What if?" But these are the exact questions that lead to breakthroughs.

Remember that every major human advancement started with someone being annoyingly curious. From penicillin to smartphones to self-driving cars – curiosity made it possible. So don't judge curious people too harshly. And most importantly, don't judge yourself for being curious. It might just be your greatest asset.

***

The Curious Carpenter

By now, you might be wondering what the old carpenter from the start of this chapter has to do with everything else we've discussed. Here is the answer: the carpenter failed to build a great house because he lacked curiosity and motivation. His mind was elsewhere, and so was his effort. If he had known from the outset that the house was for himself and his family, the entire story would have changed. Suddenly, he would have paid attention to every detail, crafted every corner with precision, and poured his heart into every nail and beam.

The carpenter's story reminds us that true success isn't built with obligation – it's built with curiosity. Without curiosity, you build houses. With curiosity, you build homes.

***

The Rule of Curiosity:

Follow your curiosity. Focus your efforts on activities that genuinely interest you and eliminate the ones that don't.

Chapter 2

Fooled by Talent

Talent is nothing more than a pursued interest.

Bob Ross

The Tale of the Two Eagles

Once upon a time, there was a king who owned two magnificent eagles in the royal garden. Every day, he admired their beauty as they perched on the branch of the tallest tree. But over time, he noticed something odd: one eagle soared high into the sky, its wings cutting gracefully through the air, while the other barely lifted off before returning to its familiar branch.

Puzzled by the reluctance of one eagle to fly higher, the king sent word throughout the kingdom, offering a substantial reward to anyone who could make the eagle join its companion in the lofty heights. Many people came and tried their best, but the eagle always returned to the branch shortly after taking flight.

One day, however, the king witnessed a remarkable sight: both eagles were soaring high in the sky, their wings outstretched. Intrigued, the king sought to find out how this had been achieved and discovered that it was a simple farmer who had found the solution.

When the king asked the farmer how he had succeeded where so many others had failed, the farmer replied, "Your Majesty, I did nothing extraordinary. I simply cut off the branch where the eagle liked to perch. With no branch to return to, the eagle had no choice but to join its companion in the sky."

The king was impressed by the farmer's ingenious solution and rewarded him generously. He realized that by removing the illusions that hold us back, we unlock our ability to soar.

***

Case Study #1: Jane and the Myth of the "Right Brain"

One day, my colleague Jane confided in me about her dissatisfaction with her role as a developer and her desire for a change. She was interested in a position on the data science team I oversaw and asked about the responsibilities and skills required for a data scientist position. Recognizing Jane's exceptional qualities — her proficiency as a developer, exemplary teamwork, likable personality, and sharp intellect — I saw her as a promising candidate for the team. I enthusiastically shared the core responsibilities of the data science team, as well as the tools we used and our business objectives.

Seeing Jane's interest in data science, I encouraged her to begin preparing for a potential role switch. I offered to assist her in selecting some relevant Pluralsight videos on data science to help her get started. Jane eagerly embraced the opportunity and requested the links that very evening. The following day, she informed me that she had already watched the recommended videos, though she admitted she found the content challenging. Nonetheless, she expressed her curiosity in learning more about the field. I suggested additional resources and wished her luck on her journey.

Weeks passed. I didn't hear from her about her progress, but I didn't want to apply pressure, so I stayed silent. Eventually, though, curiosity got the better of me, and I decided to ask how her data science journey was going.

When I asked her about her progress, she sighed. "I don't think I'm cut out for data science," she admitted, her words catching me off guard. "I don't have the right kind of brain for it."

I probed further, questioning her belief that her brain shape determined her aptitude for data science. Jane reiterated her doubts, saying that catching up to those naturally talented in the field felt like an insurmountable task.

Sadly, Jane eventually abandoned her goal of switching to data science. Despite my encouragement and support, she let her self-doubt and misconceptions about talent hold her back. The tragedy was clear. She wasn't held back by a "wrong brain" – she was held back by a wrong belief.

Case Study #2: Miguel and the Trap of Natural Talent

Another friend of mine, Miguel, is a skilled backgammon player. In his youth, Miguel and his friends were obsessed with the game. They'd play for days on end at a local club, so engrossed that they'd sometimes forget to eat or sleep. "Practice makes perfect" wasn't just a saying for them – it was a way of life. Their dedication paid off.

As their skills grew, so did their accolades. The group became strong players, winning national junior championship medals year after year. But Miguel stood out from the rest. He won multiple National Champion titles in the under-16 and under-18 categories, establishing himself as one of the top junior players in the country. He was regarded as a "natural" – someone with a rare gift for backgammon.

And Miguel believed it, too.

Two decades later, Miguel is still a strong player, but he's no longer the best. While he consistently scores above 50% in tournaments, he hasn't won a single National Championship medal in the open class. Some of his old rivals – players he used to crush with ease – have overtaken him.

Curious about this, I asked him what had changed. His response was revealing.

"These guys are constantly studying the game," he said. "They memorize openings, analyze middle-game strategies, and perfect their endgame. They're way stronger now than they were back in our youth."

"So why don't you study it the same way?" I asked.

He leaned back, his smile as self-assured as ever. "Because I'm a talented player," he said, like it was the most obvious truth in the world. "Even without all that extra work, I'm still good enough to compete with them."

There it was: the trap of "natural talent." Miguel's belief in his "natural ability" had become his ceiling. While his former rivals kept leveling up through study, analysis, and strategy, Miguel remained convinced that his raw talent was enough. He hadn't realized that his early success was a result of endless practice sessions as a teenager, not just "natural ability." But now, with fewer practice hours and no structured improvement plan, his competitors had pulled ahead.

Miguel's belief in his "natural talent" was his branch. Just like the eagle, he clung to it, never realizing he could soar.

How the Myth of Talent Keeps Us Stuck

The examples of Jane and Miguel are far from rare. In fact, they represent two of the most common ways people get "fooled by talent."

The first is when people doubt themselves. They convince themselves they lack the "right brain" for a certain task or field, believing that, no matter how much effort they put in, they'll never measure up. This is Jane's story.

The second way is when people place too much faith in their "natural talent." They believe they're special, naturally gifted, and don't need to work as hard as others. This is Miguel's story.

While Jane quits too soon, Miguel refuses to grow. Both are trapped by the same myth: the myth of talent.

There's a famous Thai proverb that claims, "Talent is born, not made." The idea is that certain people are naturally gifted in specific areas, and others will never be able to catch up. But have you ever met a "naturally gifted" person who didn't also practice obsessively?

What the Masters Say About Talent

If talent were truly the key to success, you'd expect the world's greatest performers to emphasize its importance. But that's not what they say. When the best in the world talk about success, they rarely mention talent. They talk about effort, strategy, and persistence. Michael Jordan, arguably the greatest basketball player of all time, once remarked, "Talent wins games, but teamwork and intelligence win championships." Chess legend Viktor Korchnoi went even further, claiming that talent accounts for just 5% of success, with the remaining 95% coming from hard work. Composer Irving Berlin had a similar perspective, pointing out that talent is just a starting point. And then there's author Dean Koontz, who argued that everyone has some kind of talent that, with effort, can lead to success. Across every field – sports, music, literature, and chess – the message is clear: Hard work wins.

But quotes alone aren't proof. As compelling as these statements are, they're still just opinions. So, let's turn to the evidence.

What the Science Says About Talent

Geoffrey Colvin, in his book "Talent is Overrated," argues that innate talent is not the driving force behind elite performance. Drawing on extensive research, he shows that consistent hard work and deliberate practice are the true differentiators between elite performers and everyone else.

This concept, known as "deliberate practice," was also popularized by Anders Ericsson, the researcher behind the famous "10,000-hour rule" (though that rule is often misinterpreted). The key insight is this: greatness doesn't come from talent or doing the same thing over and over again – it comes from focused, intense practice aimed at overcoming specific weaknesses.

And what do scientists say about mental talent? Let's start with the definitions. Talent is commonly defined as a natural ability to excel in a particular area, implying that skills acquired through hard work or instruction are not considered talent. Talent can't be learned or taught, which means it's something you're born with. The only other explanation would be that talent somehow miraculously appears in one's life without any intentional effort on their part. While there have been numerous claims of people suddenly acquiring talents or even superpowers — such as healing all diseases or communicating with the deceased — it is important to emphasize that none of this has been backed by scientific evidence. Therefore, when discussing talent, we refer to people with natural abilities believed to have been present since birth or shortly thereafter. Is there any evidence of the existence of talent defined as such? Is anyone born with "a chess brain" or "a math brain"?

The evidence doesn't support it. While physical traits (like height or flexibility) undeniably impact performance in sports, there's no conclusive proof that cognitive talents — like "natural logic" or "natural musical genius" — exist at birth.

Instead, research suggests that skills like chess, music, and programming are developed through practice and experience, not something people are born with. Yes, genetics may influence certain cognitive traits like memory capacity or processing speed, but these factors alone don't create prodigies, nor do they prevent anyone from becoming one. There is no gene for "chess talent" or "math talent." Your ability to play chess, compose music, or code software is determined by your experiences and how much effort you put into deliberate practice. The truth is, you're not born with a "math brain" or a "chess brain." But you can build one.

The Myths of Mozart and Magnus

People often point to "child prodigies" as proof that mental talent plays a significant role. Two names come up time and time again: Wolfgang Amadeus Mozart and Magnus Carlsen. Mozart composed his first pieces at age five, while Carlsen became a chess Grandmaster at 13. If they aren't proof of "natural talent," then what is?

The first counter-argument is that if Mozart and Carlsen had some kind of "super brain," wouldn't they be talented in significantly more areas? Wouldn't Mozart have been a chess prodigy too? Wouldn't Carlsen be composing symphonies? Yet, they showed little "talent" outside of their main playing field.

The way this question is typically answered by the proponents of "talent", is that their "talent" wasn't broad — it was specific to one field. They don't consider talent as something present across a wide spectrum of fields. But if we define talent this narrowly, it's clear their brilliance wasn't "natural" at all.

Mozart's early exposure to music came from watching his sister's music lessons. His curiosity was sparked at a young age, and that spark fueled thousands of hours of deliberate practice. He didn't suddenly "know music" — he learned it through constant exposure and rigorous training under his father, Leopold Mozart, who was a prominent composer and music teacher.

The same goes for Magnus Carlsen. While it's true that Carlsen solved puzzles at a very young age, this wasn't because of some "genius chess brain." His father was a chess enthusiast who introduced him to the game at an early age. Carlsen's early exposure to chess triggered curiosity, and that curiosity drove him to practice. It wasn't long before he was dedicating himself to hours of deliberate study and training, eventually reaching Grandmaster status at 13.

Both Mozart and Carlsen were called prodigies, but in reality, they were kids with curiosity, opportunity, and thousands of hours of practice. It was not talent that allowed them to reach their goals.

The Myth of Mental Talent

Yet, despite the overwhelming evidence, people still believe in the power of "natural talent." Why is that?

Part of it comes from the mystique that surrounds certain fields. Disciplines like science, programming, machine learning, and mind sports are seen as fields reserved for "the exceptionally smart." People in these fields are seen as having special minds — brains that are somehow different from everyone else.

I've been fortunate to operate in several of these "smart people only" fields, and I've found that being part of this seemingly elusive group can indeed enhance one's perceived intelligence. Many people have shown respect toward me simply because I have some ability to navigate these exclusive domains.

However, I would like to reveal a secret that might surprise you: the "smart people only" fields are an illusion. 95% of the people working in them don't see themselves as "special." They don't think they're smarter or more talented than everyone else. The other 5% are just narcissists.

The Evolutionary Trap

The other part comes from our evolutionary history. Over the course of 300,000 years of Homo sapiens' evolution, humans have learned the importance of conserving energy. Back when our ancestors lived in the wild, survival depended on being efficient with energy. If you wasted it, you'd be lion food.

This evolutionary lesson is still hardwired into us today. We avoid unnecessary effort whenever possible. And since the human brain itself uses an enormous amount of energy (around 20% of our total energy), it's no surprise that the brain is always looking for shortcuts. Instead of working hard, it convinces us not to give our best effort. Instead of confronting challenges, it tells us to stay in our comfort zone. It's not laziness, it's survival.

How the Concept of Talent Was Born

Given our natural tendency to save energy whenever possible, it was only a matter of time before some creative mind invented the concept of talent. They just didn't have any other justification for their laziness. Talent isn't a "real thing"; it's a story we tell ourselves to justify failure.

We always look for easy ways out, and hiding behind the lack of (or too much of) talent gives us this opportunity. The more difficult the challenge, the more time and effort is required to overcome it. Whether it be data science, backgammon, or any other skill, mastering it is hard. It takes a lot of energy and requires a committed person to tackle the challenges on the way to significant self-improvement. Most people are not that dedicated. Unless they see immediate progress, they tend to give up, blaming their perceived lack of talent for their shortcomings. It's such a trap, talent. It's one of the biggest and most dangerous lies ever told. It's a lie that fools us into failure.

Back to Jane and Miguel

> *All our dreams can come true if we have the courage to pursue them.*
>
> **Walt Disney**

This brings us back to the stories of Jane and Miguel. Jane thought she wasn't smart enough for data science, so she quit. Miguel believed his "natural talent" was enough to compete, so he stopped improving. What do they have in common?

They were both fooled by the same myth: talent.

Jane's belief that she lacked "the right brain" was a convenient excuse to avoid discomfort. After all, if you believe you don't have "the right brain," then failure isn't your fault; it's your brain's fault.

Miguel's belief in his "natural talent" was also an excuse — just in the opposite direction. He believed he was already good enough, so he had no reason to put in extra effort. If you're already great, why bother practicing?

Both Jane and Miguel missed the truth: success has never been about talent. It's about curiosity, effort, and persistence.

If Jane had believed in effort over talent, she'd be thriving as a data scientist today. If Miguel had realized that his early success wasn't "talent" but deliberate practice disguised as talent, he'd be a National Champion by now. Yet, they ended up on the couch (or on the branch) doing nothing and achieving nothing.

They had everything they needed to succeed, but they got fooled by talent.

The Rule of Talent:

Assume that talent does not exist. It's just an excuse to justify a lack of effort and a tendency to quit.

Why does it work? Because the belief in talent gives people a convenient excuse to quit. If you think you lack "the right brain" or "the natural ability," you'll give up when things get hard. But if you abandon the concept of talent entirely, you'll stop looking for excuses and start focusing on improvement.

> *Talent is cheaper than table salt. What separates the talented individual from the successful one is hard work.*
>
> **Stephen King**

Every new challenge comes with struggle. The early stages of learning are slow, awkward, and painful. It is easy to fall into the trap of believing that your struggles are caused by lack of talent. And if you convince yourself that you cannot succeed, failure will likely follow — not from lack of ability, but from lack of belief.

When you stop believing in talent, you realize that the first steps are hard for everyone. No one becomes a master overnight. There's no "natural" chess player. There's no "natural" data scientist. The experts just have the experience. You will have it too. There's no reason to doubt your potential or feel disheartened.

***

Back to the Eagles

Just like the two eagles in the story at the beginning of this chapter, each of us has the potential to soar to great heights. But here's the catch: The branch is "talent" — a perch of false comfort, stopping us from striving for the heights we're capable of reaching. If you believe in talent and convince yourself that the branch is the limit, then the branch is indeed the limit. The moment you stop believing in talent, you cut the branch and you're free to soar.

***

The Rule of Talent:

Assume that talent does not exist. It's just an excuse to justify a lack of effort and a tendency to quit.

Chapter 3

The Comfort Zone Con

When you're in flow, you're not chasing success. Success is chasing you.

Author

Sofie and the Snowy Quest for Dreamies

During my friend's business trips, her cat Sofie would stay with me. It didn't take long to discover her greatest love in life: Dreamies treats. No matter how full her belly was, there was always room for those irresistible little snacks. Over time, we established a routine. Sofie would head to a specific kitchen cabinet and paw at the door, her unmistakable signal that it was time for her beloved Dreamies.

Being the princess of the house (and fully aware of it), Sofie commanded attention. I even rearranged my workspace to be in the kitchen during her stays so I could attend to her whims without delay. Each time I heard the soft scraping of her paw on the cabinet, I knew exactly what she wanted — and, of course, I obliged.

One winter day, the world outside was transformed by a heavy snowfall. Fluffy white layers covered the ground, stacking up to dozens of centimeters. Sofie, ever the curious explorer, trotted to the terrace door, eager to go outside. But as soon as I cracked the door open, an icy gust of air rushed in. Her enthusiasm vanished, and she promptly turned back inside.

That's when an idea struck me. I decided to test Sofie's senses — her vision, to be precise. I took one of her precious Dreamies treats and placed them on a stone, several meters away from the terrace. She sat silently, gazing out at the snow. Would she notice it? Could she spot it from there?

I watched intently as she hardly moved, her eyes scanning the snowy landscape. Minutes passed. I began to wonder if the challenge was too difficult. But then, her eyes sharpened, and her ears perked up. She'd spotted it. Her gaze locked onto the distant stone. With renewed purpose, she tapped on the door, signaling me to open it.

I opened the door, and Sofie stepped cautiously onto the snowy terrace. The cold was no match for her resolve. Her paws sank into the snow, and at first, she seemed unsure of her footing. But she didn't give up. Slowly, methodically, she pressed forward, taking small, deliberate steps. Each time the snow got too deep, she adjusted her path, navigating around the thicker patches like a seasoned explorer. Her determination was undeniable.

After significant effort (and a few near missteps) Sofie finally reached her prize. She snatched up the Dreamies treat with a triumphant little chomp. Mission accomplished. Her return journey was faster, driven by the satisfaction of victory. Back inside, she groomed herself, as if she had just completed a grand adventure. And in a way, she had.

My initial goal had been to test Sofie's vision, but what I witnessed was something far more compelling. Here was a cat who faced the cold, navigated obstacles, and still claimed her reward. It's true that sometimes, the journey itself becomes the story we remember. But as I watched Sofie lounge comfortably on the warm couch, I realized something: the myths we tell ourselves about "earning" success often lead us on much colder, longer journeys than necessary.

***

The Comfort Zone Myth

Most that you've been taught about comfort zones is a lie.

Everyone says that growth happens outside your comfort zone. Motivational posters tell us this. Corporate trainers repeat it like gospel. It's become a dogma — a "truth" you aren't allowed to question.

But what if it's all wrong?

Think about it. If leaving your comfort zone is all it takes to succeed, then every uncomfortable experience should make you better. But does it? Did that awkward networking event you forced yourself to attend turn you into a master networker? Did that one "uncomfortable conversation" at work make you an expert in confrontation? Probably not.

And yet, we cling to the myth. Why? Because slick posters and celebrity soundbites seduce us with feel-good promises. They make us believe that pain leads to growth. But that's the con.

Tere Arigo says, "The hardest thing to do is leave your comfort zone. But you have to let go of the life you're familiar with and take the risk to live the life you dream about." English actor Benedict Cumberbatch echoes this idea, describing stepping out of one's comfort zone as challenging but deeply rewarding. Ray Bennett reinforces it, emphasizing that taking risks and being honest about what we want is crucial for growth.

It sounds noble, doesn't it? But does it work?

I was once a believer. For years, I searched for the "key to success," and at one moment I assumed stepping outside my comfort zone was the answer. So I tested it. Not once, not twice — but three times. I created a personal growth challenge and forced myself to do things I wouldn't normally do. Here are the three "brilliant" growth experiments that absolutely, 100% failed to change my life.

1. 6 a.m. running — because "all successful people wake up early"
2. Swimming — because I'm terribly discomfortable swimming and "embrace discomfort" is apparently a life philosophy now

3. Cold showers – because some random guy on the internet swore it would "change my life forever."

Experiment #1: 6 a.m. Running
I enjoy running, but waking up at 6 a.m. to do it? Not so much. The plan was to wake up early, lace up my shoes, and run 5 to 10 kilometers before starting my day. It sounded productive and "growth-minded," but in practice, it was torture. After 12 runs, I quit. I told myself I'd try again later. I never did.

Experiment #2: Swimming
I'm not a swimmer, but I convinced myself that battling something I struggle with would "build character." Each time, I had to mentally psych myself up. Watching "real swimmers" show off their butterfly strokes and catching the eyes of their crushes didn't help. When I tried the same, I was flailing around, looking more like I was trying to survive a shipwreck, and only catching the eyes of the lifeguards. I gave up.

Experiment #3: Cold Showers
The concept is simple: no warm water allowed. Just ice-cold water, every day. Allegedly, this builds mental toughness, boosts energy, and provides health benefits. I gave it a try. Once. Then I tried again. Twice. After that? Nope. I saw no point in freezing myself every morning when I had the luxury of warm water. I stopped. No regrets.

None of these experiments lasted long. I didn't become a "mental toughness warrior." I didn't unlock my "hidden potential." So, what went wrong? Why didn't all that discomfort pay off like everyone promised it would?

The Reality of Comfort Zones

Contrary to popular belief, being outside your comfort zone isn't inherently valuable. In psychology, a "comfort zone" is a state of control and ease. Leaving it means stepping into discomfort and uncertainty — and there's nothing magical about either of those states. Growth doesn't come from discomfort itself. Growth comes from what you *learn* while navigating discomfort.

So, why does this myth persist? It's simple: people often notice success follows moments when they step outside their comfort zone. It's an easy but flawed conclusion to think one caused the other. But correlation isn't causation. Stepping outside your comfort zone doesn't *cause* success. Discomfort alone doesn't create growth — learning does. It always has.

The same misconception surrounds failure. It's true that success often comes after failure, but it's not failure itself that drives success. It's the *learning* that happens after failure. People fail, they learn, and later, they succeed. But if you fail and learn nothing, all you've done is fail.

Self-improvement authors love to boast that they "failed their way to success." But that's an illusion. Nobody fails their way to success. You *learn* your way to success.

Neither failure nor being outside your comfort zone is inherently good. If you fail but learn nothing, you gain nothing. If you leave your comfort zone but learn nothing, you gain nothing. Growth doesn't come from discomfort or failure — it comes from reflection, analysis, and applying the lessons you've learned. Without that, discomfort is just suffering, and failure is just failure.

Why We Overvalue Discomfort

"But discomfort and failure cause us to learn," claim the fans of "step outside your comfort zone." Well, they're wrong again. While it's true that people often learn more from failures and discomfort than from successes or comfortable situations, it's not the discomfort or failing itself that drives learning. It comes down to human nature.

When we succeed, we rarely reflect on *why* it happened. Success feels good, so we move on and celebrate. But when we fail or face discomfort, our brains go into overdrive, trying to make sense of what went wrong. Painful experiences are far more memorable than successful ones, so we reflect on them more deeply. And it's this reflection — *not* the discomfort itself — where the real learning happens.

The confusion comes from this simple pattern: Discomfort → Reflection/Learning → Growth.

People mistakenly think the first step is the key ingredient. It's not. Discomfort doesn't cause growth any more than rain alone makes crops grow. It's the sunlight, soil, and care that do the real work.

If you want to accelerate your growth, don't chase discomfort. Chase *analysis*. If you can reflect on your successes as thoroughly as your failures, you'll unlock a powerful advantage. And if you can reflect on the lessons learned inside your comfort zone, you'll realize you don't need discomfort to grow.

The Takeaway

What does this mean for my three failed experiments? They were destined to fail from the start. As we discussed in Chapter 1, if you force yourself to do something you hate, with no clear purpose or goal, you're unlikely to stick with it. I didn't need early morning runs, cold swims, or icy showers to grow. What I needed was to follow my curiosity.

Instead of forcing myself to run at 6 a.m., I could have explored my curiosity about physical fitness. Instead of swimming in cold water for the sake of discomfort, I could have pursued an interest in swimming techniques. Instead of enduring cold showers, I could have asked myself, "What other mental toughness exercises would actually excite me?"

It doesn't mean that stepping outside your comfort zone is wrong — getting stuck there is. If you're unhappy with life and need a significant change, you might need to step out, but not to chase discomfort. You step out to chase change. The goal isn't to stay outside your comfort zone forever. The goal is to expand it, so the activities that once felt difficult become part of your "normal."

From Discomfort to Mastery: How I Mastered Quoridor

After sharing a string of failed experiments, I don't want to sound like a bitter old whiner. So, let's shift gears and look at a success story — my journey to mastering Quoridor. This project illustrates how strategically moving in and out of your comfort zone can lead to mastery.

Unlike my cold showers or 6 a.m. runs, I was genuinely curious about Quoridor. That curiosity was my starting fuel. I also knew that success in mind sports had nothing to do with talent, which gave me two essential pieces of the success puzzle. What remained was figuring out how to leave my comfort zone strategically — and, just as importantly, how to return to it.

Taking on new challenges often requires stepping out of your comfort zone, and that was certainly the case with Quoridor. Progress was slow at first. I was in unfamiliar territory, and my initial approach wasn't exactly optimal. If I had been fooled by the "talent trap," I might have convinced myself that I just didn't have the "talent" for it and quit before making any real progress. But I knew better. Instead of quitting, I focused on how to make my process more efficient.

I developed a strategy. Every evening, I scheduled three dedicated hours for Quoridor practice. I set a strict rule for myself: analyze every game before playing the next one. This simple rule turned out to be a game-changer. It forced me to reflect on my mistakes, spot patterns, and identify new tactics. Over time, I discovered better, faster ways to study and improve. My approach to Quoridor wasn't just improving — my approach to learning itself was evolving.

Then something incredible happened. What was once uncomfortable and difficult gradually became smooth and automatic. I had successfully expanded my comfort zone. Playing Quoridor wasn't outside my comfort zone anymore. It had become as natural as brushing my teeth. It didn't feel like work anymore. It felt like gliding downhill with a tailwind – effortless and unstoppable. I had entered the state that athletes call "being in the zone" and writers call "flow."

Flow: The Ultimate Comfort Zone

Flow is peak performance – a state where every action is optimized, every step is precise, and nothing feels forced. You're operating within your comfort zone, fully aware of your goals, and you know exactly how to achieve them. You're no longer guessing or fumbling. You're in control.

Think about simple tasks like brushing your teeth or making your morning coffee. Over time, you've perfected these routines so thoroughly that they require zero mental effort. You know where the toothpaste is, you know exactly how much to squeeze, and you can probably brush your teeth with your eyes closed. Making coffee is no different. You know where to find the beans, how to operate the coffee machine, and where to grab your favorite mug. Everything is second nature. In the flow state time vanishes, doubt disappears, and only the task remains.

Now, contrast this with someone trying to brush their teeth for the first time (a toddler) or someone making coffee in a stranger's kitchen. Suddenly, every little action requires extra time and thought. Everything takes longer, mistakes are made, and it feels more frustrating.

It is evident that operating within a flow state is far more effective than struggling outside your comfort zone. Therefore, it is advisable to always seek opportunities to transition from the latter to the former. When you're in flow, you're not chasing success. Success is chasing you.

The Surprising Role of Routine

Want flow? Start with routine. It's the launchpad for peak performance. Routine creates the conditions for flow and is often a necessary step in achieving it.

Yet, routines are often misunderstood and unfairly criticized. People claim to hate routine, equating it with stagnation or being stuck in your comfort zone. But that's a shallow interpretation. In reality, routines are one of the most powerful tools for success.

Take fitness, for example. Imagine you go to the gym for two intense months and then never return. Sure, you'll see some progress, but the moment you stop, your gains disappear. If you want sustainable fitness, you have to make it a part of your daily life. And that's exactly what fitness enthusiasts do. They don't view gym time as a challenge or an adventure — they view it as a routine. It's part of their day, like eating lunch or brushing their teeth.

Here's the key: When a routine exists outside your comfort zone, it's hard to maintain. My cold showers and 6 a.m. runs were perfect examples of this. They remained outside my comfort zone, so I abandoned them.

But when routines become part of your comfort zone, they stick. Quoridor, for me, became a daily ritual. It wasn't something I had to push through — it was something I looked forward to. The same goes for any routine you genuinely enjoy. True football (soccer) fans never complain about watching their favorite team play every week. For them, it's not a chore — it's a weekly ritual filled with hope, heartbreak, and questionable referee decisions.

Here's the takeaway: Nobody really hates routines. People hate boring routines. Nobody hates the routine of cashing a paycheck.

If you build routines around activities you love or are genuinely curious about, they don't feel like routines. They feel like flow. That's why the best performers know how to master both. They follow routines to reduce mental load, and they engage in flow for peak performance.

The Rule of the Comfort Zone:

Don't live outside your comfort zone — expand it. Aim for flow, not struggle.

Why does it work? You are inefficient outside your comfort zone. Discomfort for the sake of discomfort is pointless. Efficiency, especially in the flow state, can be achieved in an environment where you feel in control.

Jane's Journey

Let's check back in with Jane, the developer from the previous chapter, who is still chasing her dream of becoming a data scientist. Her story perfectly illustrates the impact of the three rules we've discussed so far.

1. The Rule of Curiosity

Jane was inspired by the work of her data science colleagues. She admired the kind of problems they solved and saw their tasks as more enjoyable and fulfilling. This indicates a genuine curiosity for data science, which satisfies the first rule. Her initial spark of interest was strong, and she had the drive to learn more.

2. The Rule of Talent

But things took a turn here. As Jane started studying data science, she didn't see the rapid progress she'd hoped for. She misinterpreted this as a sign that she "didn't have the right brain" for the field. This was a classic example of falling into the talent trap. Had she followed the rule of talent — which tells us that talent is a myth — she would have recognized that slow progress is perfectly normal in any new endeavor. Instead of giving up, she would have stayed the course, knowing that effort and persistence always trump talent.

3. The Rule of the Comfort Zone

Now, let's imagine a better version of Jane's story. Let's assume she didn't fall for the talent trap and continued her pursuit of data science. This brings us to the third rule: Don't live outside your comfort zone – expand it.

Jane wasn't thrilled with her job as a developer, so stepping out of her comfort zone wasn't just brave – it was strategic. Had she been perfectly happy as a developer, there would have been no reason to step out of her comfort zone at all. But she wasn't happy, and she was curious about something that lay outside her comfort zone (data science). This is a textbook scenario for when it's wise to leave your comfort zone.

When Jane first started learning data science, she was clearly outside her comfort zone. Her productivity was low, her progress was slow, and her self-doubt was probably at an all-time high. This is perfectly normal. In the early stages, curiosity often compensates for slow progress, keeping you motivated despite the challenges. Sometimes, that curiosity alone is enough to naturally pull you back into your comfort zone, bringing a new skill or knowledge along for the ride (in Jane's case – data science). Other times, though, curiosity isn't enough. When that happens, deliberate effort is required. And if you can't expand your comfort zone naturally, the best way to force it is through routine.

Here's how Jane could structure it:

- Set aside a fixed, daily time slot for studying data science – for example, 9 p.m. every evening.
- Keep the sessions short and achievable. Even 30-60 minutes is enough if done consistently.

- Attach a small reward to the routine. After a successful study session, she could reward herself with a cup of gourmet coffee, a tasty snack, or 15 minutes of entertainment.

With this approach, Jane would have built a rock-solid habit and turned data science from a daunting mystery into a daily ritual. Over time, she would notice that data science no longer feels unfamiliar or overwhelming. It would become a natural part of her daily life — part of her comfort zone.

When you create a routine for something, it moves from "unknown and stressful" to "known and automatic." This process is the essence of expanding your comfort zone. With dedication and consistency, the discomfort of learning a new skill fades, and what once felt like a burden becomes a source of joy. The better you get at something, the more fun it becomes.

The Sofie Lesson

Wondering how Sofie's story relates to your success journey? It's simple: She trudged through the snow to reach the Dreamies — but she didn't have to. She didn't have to leave her comfort zone at all. Sometimes, we glorify struggle when simpler, smarter options are right in front of us. Why trudge through snow when a paw-swipe will do?

***

The Rule of the Comfort Zone:

Don't live outside your comfort zone — expand it. Aim for flow, not struggle.

Chapter 4

The Red Ferrari Effect

What could we accomplish if we knew we could not fail?
Eleanor Roosevelt

The Genius Disguise: Outsmarting the Impossible Question

Albert Einstein was traveling from city to city, delivering lectures on his groundbreaking theory of relativity. It was a rigorous schedule, and one evening, just before yet another talk, he let out a weary sigh.

"Ugh, I'm so tired of giving the same lecture over and over," he groaned to his driver. "I wish I could just sit back and relax for once."

The driver, who bore a striking resemblance to Einstein, had a mischievous grin on his face. "You know, Professor, I think I've got an idea. I've been to so many of your lectures that I've memorized every word. I don't understand a thing, but I could recite it in my sleep. Why don't I pretend to be you? You can sit in the back and take it easy."

Einstein's eyes lit up with playful mischief. "That's brilliant! Let's do it."

So, they swapped clothes — the driver donning Einstein's iconic suit, and Einstein putting on the driver's simple uniform and cap. With their uncanny resemblance, nobody suspected a thing.

The driver-turned-"Einstein" took the stage and delivered the lecture perfectly, his delivery smooth and confident. The crowd was none the wiser, captivated by the performance. But just as he was basking in his success, a man in the audience stood up and asked a highly technical question — one that would stump even a seasoned physicist.

The driver froze. The room fell silent. All eyes were on him. He had seconds to react. But then, with impeccable composure, he smirked and said, "Ah, that's an excellent question. In fact, it's so simple that even my driver in the back can answer it!"

And just like that, Einstein stepped in to handle the question.

***

The Departure of Ekaterina

You lean back in your plush office chair, gazing out the window at the sweeping view from YourCompany's headquarters. As CEO and founder, it's been another long but productive day. The weight of leadership rests on your shoulders, but for a brief moment, you allow yourself to relax.

A knock at the door pulls you from your thoughts. It's Ekaterina, the Head of Marketing. She stands at the doorway, her fingers fidgeting with the corner of her notebook. Her eyes avoid yours, darting to the floor for a moment before locking in. Something isn't right.

You swallow, buying a few seconds of time. "What's on your mind?" you ask, your tone calm but alert.

Ekaterina hesitates, glancing at the floor before looking you in the eye. Finally, she speaks. "I've made the decision to leave YourCompany."

The words hit you like a punch to the gut. For a moment, you're speechless.

"Why?" you ask, trying to keep your voice steady.

She takes a breath and begins to explain. Her reasons are thoughtful and well-articulated — a combination of personal growth, new challenges, and opportunities she feels she can't pass up.

In the days that follow, you and Helen, YourCompany's Head of Human Resources, try to change her mind. You meet with her, listen carefully, and offer counterarguments, but

Ekaterina remains firm. Her mind is made up. Eventually, you accept the reality: she's leaving.

Helen reminds you to prepare a farewell speech for Ekaterina's last day. It will be a chance to recognize her contributions and show the team how much she meant to the company. It's also an opportunity to leave a lasting impression — on her and on everyone else. It's a critical moment — one that defines how leaders are remembered. And like all crucial moments, it can play out in more than one way.

Three Paths, Three Outcomes

What happens next is entirely in your hands. Your task is clear: deliver a farewell speech that acknowledges Ekaterina's contributions, strengthens her connection to YourCompany, and leaves her with positive feelings that may one day inspire her to return.

In real life, you only get one shot to deliver this speech. If you fumble it, there's no redo. But let's imagine you had three tries. Here's how it could unfold...

Scenario One: Underestimating the Task

You have agreed with Ekaterina that her last day will be October 31st. On October 3rd, exactly four weeks before her departure, Helen, the Head of HR, reminded you to prepare a farewell speech for the 31st, but you dismissed the task. You've given farewell speeches before and feel it's unnecessary to devote time to it, especially with other pressing matters at hand. Besides, four weeks is an eternity, right?

Time flies quickly in the corporate world, and before you knew it, October 31st had arrived. Helen pops into your office, reminding you that it's Ekaterina's last day — also her birthday. When you show little interest, she takes it upon herself to buy flowers for Ekaterina. You hide the flowers under your desk and, feeling there's still time, dive back into preparing documents for the upcoming board meeting.

Suddenly, it's 4pm – time for your farewell speech. As per tradition, the small company gathers in the kitchen, including the radiant Ekaterina. At 4:05 pm, Helen rushes into your office to notify you that everyone is eagerly awaiting your arrival.

After several glances at your board meeting documents, you finally enter the kitchen at 4:15 pm. The room falls quiet. All eyes turn towards you. Your heart skips a beat. You forgot the flowers. Blood rushes to your face as you dart back to your office, hoping nobody notices. When rejoining the expectant crowd, slightly flustered, you start your farewell speech.

"My dearly beloved YourCompany heroes," you begin with your signature line that never fails to elicit laughter. It acts as a reliable icebreaker – like a comfortable old shoe, unless it's too worn out. It's a promising start, but then it hits you: you have absolutely nothing prepared.

You can't just stand there without saying anything, though, so you continue, "We have gathered here in our small, lovely kitchen area to say goodbye to Ekaterina." Everybody is still focused on you in good spirits, and you go on, "There have been some good times and ... um ... there have been some bad times ... um ... but now Ekaterina has decided to pursue new dreams." You can feel bewildered employees exchanging glances due to your confusing words. You still have no idea what to say next, so you try to wrap up before it gets any more awkward.

"Thank you, Ekaterina, for the time spent with us. We wish you all the best in your new challenges." You approach Ekaterina and give her a half-hearted hug along with the flowers, turning to Helen, "Cut the cake," you say, sealing your fate as the guy who made his best employee feel like an afterthought on her birthday.

***

There's Ekaterina, the unwavering Head of Marketing, who has devoted four years to propelling YourCompany towards success. She has dedicated countless late nights and tireless efforts to meet deadlines, never once complaining during demanding campaigns. Is this really the farewell speech she deserves?

Certainly not. Not even close. It's a downright failure and a disgrace. If your goal was to ensure Ekaterina never returns to YourCompany, congratulations – you're off to a great start. You've just ruined the birthday of your most valued colleague. Where did things go wrong?

At its core, the issue stems from underestimating the task and taking it too lightly. This often results in oversimplification, where critical details are overlooked or dismissed. Unsurprisingly, this approach rarely produces success. Instead, it invites negative consequences – lost games, disappointed stakeholders, and strained relationships. In this case, it leaves behind confused colleagues and a disheartened Ekaterina.

Scenario Two: Overestimating the Challenge

You have agreed with Ekaterina that her last day will be October 31st. Helen reminds you on October 3rd about the farewell speech, and panic sets in. Public speaking is not your forte, and you dread the idea. Still, you recognize the importance of the farewell speech and don't want to disappoint her. Although the idea of delegating the speech momentarily crosses your mind, you understand that as her direct boss, this is your responsibility. It's four weeks; you have time to prepare.

Over the next month, you sit down to work on the speech, gathering ideas and reflecting on Ekaterina's successes. You dive into her long list of tasks in Jira, trying to compile a list of her work-related accomplishments. Conceding to your limitations in public speaking, you decide to keep the speech factual and somewhat shallow, focusing on her achievements. You intend to read it verbatim from a script, setting your sights on delivering A speech rather than THE speech.

On October 31st, you arrive at the office, the speech carefully penned on paper. Understanding your nerves might sabotage your performance, you delegate handling the flowers and cake to Helen, minimizing your role in the farewell.

At 4 p.m., everyone gathers in the kitchen for the farewell – a radiant Ekaterina is among the crowd. Feeling your hands tremble, you search your pocket for the speech you prepared. The paper isn't there. It's in your office. Panic rises in your chest like a wave. You rush back to grab it, but the moment you return, every eye is locked on you. Taking a deep breath, you kick off with:

"My dearly beloved YourCompany heroes! Dear Ekaterina! It has been an incredible journey of over four years since you joined our company, elevating our marketing decisions to unprecedented heights. It's time to reflect on your remarkable successes and accomplishments during your time at YourCompany." Starting with your meticulously crafted list, you keep your gaze lowered at the paper instead of connecting with your audience. With a voice like a "text-to-speech robot," you recite each feat:

"From the successful launch of our inaugural TV campaign in Portugal – which remarkably doubled our operations in six months – to rectifying a critical flaw in our marketing acquisition model that had persisted for years..."

You don't realize it yourself, but you sound like narrating an instruction manual. As you continue, you notice a few employees checking their phones, some exchanging whispers. You start to feel your speech losing its audience. Skipping some of the lengthy praise, you rush to the end:

"Your work has been commendable. I hope you find as much success in your new challenges. Thank you for your invaluable contributions, and best of luck."

You walk over to Ekaterina, offering her a lackluster hug along with the flowers, then turn to Helen and say, "Helen, it's time to cut the cake!"

***

Compared to Scenario One, your performance here was undeniably stronger. You made a commendable effort to highlight Ekaterina's accomplishments, and your praise was both thoughtful and generous. Unlike in Scenario One, you wisely avoided mentioning any negative moments. Yet, despite these improvements, the speech still fell short of brilliance.

Your delivery felt like reading a dry report. While you offered relevant accolades, the speech lacked vitality and emotional resonance, rendering it dull and focused only on the work aspect. It was boring.

The pitfall here was overestimating the difficulty of your task while underestimating your abilities. Your initial doubts clouded your approach, leading to a safely mediocre performance. As discussed in earlier chapters, you can only soar if you refuse to impose limits on yourself. When you underestimate your capabilities, you hinder your potential. While Ekaterina may not be upset with your speech, she's left unimpressed. You didn't ruin her day as you did in Scenario One, but you certainly didn't make it special. Additionally, you focused only on her last workday of the job, overlooking that it was also her birthday.

But what if you get it right? What if you find the perfect balance? Here's how that moment might play out.

Scenario Three: Striking the Right Balance

You and Ekaterina have agreed that her last day will be October 31. However, long before that (the evening she resigns) you begin preparing her farewell speech, reflecting on cherished memories: entertaining conversations, comforting walks, skiing trips, and even more peculiar ice-skating endeavors. Your connection has surpassed mere colleagues, evolving into a genuine friendship. You recall quirky details, such as her birth in Yekaterinburg, aptly named "Ekaterina's City," and how her departure coincides with her 34th birthday.

You ponder significant transitions in her life: developing her own app, becoming a UNICEF ambassador, and the loss of her father. You also acknowledge moments of tension in the office, reflecting on interactions that may have contributed to her decision to move on.

Despite the challenges, Ekaterina's compassion and positive demeanor earned her the nickname "Angel" from colleagues, and she was awarded "Colleague of the Year." You recognize her undeniable impact on the team and workplace.

On October 3, Helen reminds you about the speech, but you're almost finished. You practice meticulously, committing each word to memory. New ideas keep flowing, allowing your speech to evolve organically. By October 31, you're fully prepared and confident.

At 4 p.m., the team gathers in the kitchen. Ekaterina's radiance illuminates the room. As the crowd quiets, all attention shifts to you.

"Dear YourCompany heroes!" you declare, using your signature phrase, but this time, you pause.

"Once upon a time, an angel left the sky and came down to Earth," you continue, captivating the audience. "Against all odds, luck brought this angel to YourCompany. Now, after four successful years, luck has turned sour, and it's time for her to spread her wings."

Turning to Ekaterina, you continue, "Dear Ekaterina, our angel." You pause for the audience to process your words. "Angel," being Ekaterina's nickname, explains your original opening lines. "Today, we celebrate not only your departure but also your birthday. As our radiant angel, it marks your 25th birthday." You give a playful nod, knowing she's 34, adding levity and ensuring her special day isn't overlooked.

"It was exactly a quarter of a century ago that your eyes first opened in the quaint city of Sverdlovsk. Angels were so rare in that city that the locals renamed it Ekaterinburg to honor you." This playful mix of fact and myth brings smiles and knowing nods.

You continue, "During your time with us, you accomplished more than many do in a lifetime. From building the Marketing team to optimizing channels with unwavering efficiency, your contributions have been instrumental. Thanks to you, we've broken records in CPA almost every quarter. And let's not forget, you brought home our prestigious Colleague of the Year award last year." There have been plenty of work talks over the years; there is no need to do anymore now. What you did in Scenario Two was overkill.

You move on: "Still, in spite of your great achievements in the office, I remember even better times with you outside of the office. I remember our talks over the dinner table in fancy restaurants and our walks afterward. We always had philosophical and existential discussions on how to save lives, how to make the world a better place, and ... whether to order octopus or salmon." The audience laughs.

"I also remember times when we went skiing ... and you repeatedly fell over ... and then you laughed at yourself." More laughter.

"I remember times when we went skating ... and I repeatedly fell over ... and then you laughed at ME." The laughter grows louder.

You continue with personal anecdotes, incorporating humor, shared memories, and a genuine appreciation for Ekaterina's character.

Then, unexpectedly, you transition to a more serious tone: "There have been so many times I have seen you laugh ... but unfortunately, there have also been times I have seen you cry." You pause, allowing the tension to build.

"During your time with us, you have had to go through some very hard times. In some cases, like losing a deeply loved family member far too early, we could have done nothing about it. In other cases, however, like conflicts and misunderstandings in the office, we certainly could have done better." You acknowledge the company's shortcomings, recognizing the pain caused.

"Nothing is more important in hard times than treating our best people with dignity. And as I reflect on those moments, I see where we could have done better. Where we SHOULD have done better. I'm using this opportunity to apologize on behalf of the entire company that during those hard times we did not treat you as well as we should have and did not support you as much as we could have. It was wrong, unfair, and hurtful. It was not what should have happened ... and you deserved none of it." You see a tear fall from Ekaterina's eye, and others in the audience are wiping their own tears.

"Our best colleague leaving us is certainly one of the low points of the company's history. It causes us to look into the mirror and ask what went wrong within the company. Over the history of YourCompany, I have seen dozens of people leaving ... but never have I felt so heartbroken."

You change your tone again, ending on a positive note. "But, after all, it's a farewell, not a funeral, so let's finish on a positive note. We have no doubt that where you will go, the sky will be bluer for you. I hope you will find happiness in your new job the same way suffering kids find happiness through your UNICEF activities. I hope you will succeed in your pursuit of saving lives and making the world a better place. And most certainly, I hope you will learn to prefer salmon over octopus." You bring the audience back to smiles and laughter.

"Thank you, Ekaterina, for those four years at YourCompany. Thank you for being the best colleague. Thank you for being a great friend. And thank you for being an angel." You go to Ekaterina, give her a hug and the flowers. Tears well up in her eyes, expressing her deep appreciation for your speech. The hug lasts a long moment as she wipes away her tears.

You have delivered the best speech of your life, making Ekaterina's special day truly memorable. The warmth and emotion filling the room is a testament to the power of your words.

Everyone approaches Ekaterina, offering hugs and well wishes. The atmosphere is thick with emotion, a mix of sadness and celebration. Nobody cares about the cake. They don't need food for their stomachs; your speech has provided enough nourishment for their souls.

***

Why were you successful in Scenario Three while failing in the previous two? The key difference was your ability to avoid being swayed by either underestimating or overestimating the challenge at hand. You approached the speech with ambition and determination, setting high goals and focusing on achieving them. You made the speech a priority, devoting your time and energy to its success. You were on a mission.

In Scenario One, you underestimated the difficulty of the task, a common reason for failure. Scenario Two highlights a less recognized but equally detrimental factor: overestimating the challenge. This brings us to the concept of the "Red Ferrari effect."

The Red Ferrari Effect

Believing in a solution paves the way to that solution.

David J. Schwartz

Reflecting on my experiences in mind sports, I've noticed that my most unexpected victories against higher-rated opponents often came when I was unaware of their high rankings. Conversely, when I knew they were rated significantly higher than me, I frequently underperformed. My perception of their superiority hindered my performance, preventing me from realizing my full potential. My mindset was essential; I could only excel when I genuinely believed in my ability to succeed.

This insight extends beyond mind sports. I realized that self-doubt significantly impacted my efforts, leading me to approach challenges with hesitance and mediocrity. I came to understand that success is intricately linked to self-belief. As I explored these reflections further, memories of watching Formula 1 races surfaced, unveiling a distinct parallel.

My fascination with Formula 1 began in the late nineties and early 2000s, a period dominated by Michael Schumacher and his iconic red Scuderia Ferrari. Schumacher's unmatched prowess on the track allowed him to consistently outpace faster cars. A key factor in his success was his competitors' tendency to falter under pressure, making costly mistakes.

The psychological impact of Schumacher's speed began to take its toll on his rivals. The mere sight of his red Ferrari in their mirrors induced panic, prompting errors that allowed him to execute passes that seemed impossible. The red Ferrari wasn't faster because it had better specs. It was faster because the drivers ahead believed it was faster — and that belief caused them to make mistakes.

I dubbed this phenomenon the "Red Ferrari effect," illustrating how perception can shape outcomes. It highlights how our beliefs about someone else's superiority can influence their actual performance, creating a self-fulfilling prophecy. If we perceive someone as better than ourselves, they are likely to perform better, even when that initial assumption might not be accurate. In the eyes of Schumacher's rivals, that red Ferrari was always a swift, threatening presence, and even if it shouldn't have overtaken them, it often did.

This example demonstrates that success is not solely about skill but also about perceived ability. Remember the story of Albert Einstein and his driver? The driver, lacking scientific knowledge, was believed by the audience to be an expert. Therefore, avoiding the "Red Ferrari effect" is as vital as not underestimating the challenge at hand.

This brings us to a pivotal question: how can we achieve this, and when should we act? I will first tackle the *how*, as it also sheds light on the *when*.

Let's use public speaking as a case in point. It's evident that you perform better when fully prepared and free from unexpected interruptions. In an ideal scenario, you have complete control over every facet of your presentation. Imagine knowing your speech thoroughly, delivering it without interruptions, and exiting the stage without fielding questions. In this context, nothing could go wrong.

Now, let's consider the possibility of audience questions. While this may still allow for a good degree of control, it introduces uncertainty. If you happen to not know the answer to a question, then you lose that control.

In the worst-case scenario, if you're thrust onto the stage with no preparation whatsoever, the scene can quickly devolve into chaos. In such cases, not only is the likelihood of your presentation being memorable drastically reduced, but if it is remembered, it's often for all the wrong reasons.

The benefits of being in control are clear. When you steer the ship, every decision aligns with your interests. Conversely, if someone else takes control, their motives may not resonate with yours, potentially leading to uncomfortable situations. Imagine if the Head of Human Resources interrupted your speech midway or put you on the spot with impulsive tasks, like telling a funny story about Ekaterina – something you are not prepared for. If you are not a particularly quick thinker, this can result in awkwardness. By taking control, we can successfully steer clear of these unpleasant scenarios and ensure that every moment showcases our strengths.

I singled out public speaking as an example because it clearly illustrates how the level of control can significantly influence outcomes. I was once your stereotypical nerd, utterly dreading public speaking and performing poorly. I fell victim to the "Red Ferrari effect," convincing myself I'd never excel at delivering speeches. Even when I tried to prepare, I often fell short. Instead of carefully planning and memorizing my talks, I would jot down a few bullet points on a sticky note and rely on that during my presentations. When I stumbled, I'd glance at the note for the next point, moving on. This approach left me feeling out of control — my goal wasn't to excel but to avoid humiliation. I settled for mediocrity, believing that dodging embarrassment was the best I could achieve. As illustrated earlier, aiming for mediocrity guarantees just that — mediocrity. I was trapped in a cycle of self-imposed failure due to the "Red Ferrari effect," accepting subpar performance as sufficient. One can never truly excel while being okay with failing.

> *Believe in yourself! Have faith in your abilities! Without humble but reasonable confidence in your own powers, you cannot be successful or happy.*
>
> **Norman Vincent Peale**

After realizing I was falling prey to the "Red Ferrari effect," I knew I had to find a solution. I pondered how to take control in challenging situations, particularly during public speaking engagements. The answer was clear: I needed to know my presentation inside out. This approach soon led to my most successful public speech to date. Since then, I've adhered to the same game plan before all my public appearances. I meticulously go through every line, committing them to memory word for word, noting when I'll pause and for how long. While this kind of memorization seems time consuming and tedious at first, the more you practice, the easier it becomes. Plus, there are unexpected benefits. I found it helpful to start rehearsing my speech even when it was still just a rough outline. As I rehearsed in my mind, new ideas emerged. By incorporating these ideas as they came to me, my presentation organically evolved.

Proper preparation becomes easier with each experience. When you succeed once, you want to feel that success again, which provides extra motivation for thorough preparation for the next opportunity. Ultimately, success breeds more success through confidence.

Success breeds more success through confidence.

Author

These days, my colleagues see me as one of the best in the game when it comes to public speaking. Little do they know that it's all due to the countless hours of practice I invest each time. Without that preparation, I would be sweating like a popsicle in the sun. I just seem proficient because I rehearse like there is no tomorrow. It almost feels like cheating, as I'm not competing on a level playing field with many others. But hey, they've got only themselves to blame for not preparing properly.

Jane's Journey

Let's explore another example of how to seize control by revisiting Jane's journey as she transitions from a developer to a data scientist. In a hypothetical scenario where she diligently follows the principles outlined in previous chapters, Jane would build a solid foundation of skills and knowledge. When she applies for a data scientist position and faces a technical interview, several scenarios are possible.

In an ideal situation, Jane might be fortunate enough to receive the interview questions in advance. This opportunity allows her to prepare thoroughly, ensuring she can provide well-structured answers and maintain full control during the discussion. By meticulously crafting her responses, she can effectively showcase her expertise without having any obstacles stand in her way.

However, it's possible advance questions are not provided. For instance, Jane may be informed only that during the interview she will be working with a dataset to create a machine-learning model for predicting specific outcomes. In such cases, seizing control becomes more challenging. Nevertheless, she can still enhance her preparedness by practicing similar modeling exercises with different datasets. While not perfect, it will allow reasonable control.

In the worst-case scenario, there may be instances where no information is given about the specifics of the interview. It's vital to acknowledge that certain circumstances limit the level of control one can exert. In these situations, rather than expending energy on futile attempts to prepare for the unknown, it may be more productive to redirect that time and effort toward more meaningful pursuits. When the opportunity to take control arises, practice diligently; otherwise, recognize that sometimes it isn't worth the effort to prepare for uncertainties.

It is essential to be in control to succeed with your event-related goals but simply knowing that isn't enough. The next ingredient of the success formula should tell us HOW to take control. Based on the above examples, you probably already understand how to do this. The trick is proper rehearsal, which creates the conditions necessary to be in control. This approach is widely utilized in show business and sports but often overlooked in daily life.

The Rule of the Red Ferrari:

Take control through rehearsal. This is how you can bring your A-game and outperform the "Red Ferrari effect."

Why does it work? You always perform better when you are in control because you avoid unpleasant surprises. Rehearsing is the best way to take control.

What's Worth Rehearsing (and What Isn't)

We have briefly touched on the fact that not everything is worth rehearsing. It's essential to identify the optimal moments for rehearsal. The worlds of show business and sports offer valuable insights into this strategic approach. In show business, actors rehearse specific scenes to ensure flawless execution during filming. The goal is not to improve overall acting skills but to deliver a captivating performance in that particular scene. Similarly, athletes practice specific scenarios that may occur in upcoming games. For example, rehearsing set plays for corner kicks in football allows each player to understand their role. The idea behind the rehearsal is to improve the team's chances of scoring from corner kicks, not to win the *Ballon d'Or*.

The main takeaway from the above is to rehearse for short-term, event-related goals, such as a weekend tennis tournament, a job interview, thesis defense, or delivering a farewell speech. Event-related goals are time-bound, imminent, and linked to specific occasions. It is unrealistic and ineffective to rehearse for broad, overarching goals like advancing in your career, completing a PhD, or refining your public speaking skills.

What was once a long-term, overarching goal can transition into a short-term, event-related goal. For example, while working on your first scientific paper, you can't realistically rehearse for earning a doctoral degree. However, as you progress and approach the thesis defense as the final hurdle, it becomes a short-term goal necessitating thorough rehearsal.

Rehearsing for everything isn't always the best idea; it can be time-consuming and not necessarily rewarding. For instance, if you're attending a job interview just for fun, with no intention of accepting the position, there's little point in preparing for it. I remember a guy who attended an interview solely because he heard they had fancy chocolates in the room. He had no relevant skills and clearly hadn't prepared. He couldn't answer a single question properly but didn't seem bothered. All he wanted was to stretch the interview long enough to enjoy two chocolates without appearing greedy. Once he finished the last piece, he suddenly became in a hurry and rushed out mid-sentence. As I showed him out, he asked if there were more positions available for him to interview for. I guess the chocolates didn't disappoint.

Deciding what's worth rehearsing can be tricky, as the value isn't always immediately obvious. Rather than over-analyzing the significance of each goal, a simpler approach is to consider whether you truly care about the outcome and whether rehearsing can lead to significant results. If both conditions are satisfied, then it is worth preparing.

Here's a list of goals where rehearsals have paid off for me:

- Public speeches and presentations: Memorize your script and rehearse until you can deliver it effortlessly.
- Leading meetings and video calls: Plan your topics and questions in advance for smoother discussions.
- Performances: Whether it's mental calculations, magic tricks, or juggling, practice makes perfect to impress your audience.
- Job interviews: Preparation is key to making a good impression and being on point, whether you're the interviewer or interviewee.
- (Mind) sports competitions: Practice sessions beforehand can greatly improve your performance.

All these goals are related to specific events that take place over a short period and are easy to prepare for.

Bringing It All Together

Rehearsal is critical for achieving event-related goals and objectives. While it may sound cliché, the truth it holds is often overlooked. Despite knowing its significance, we often struggle to find the motivation for meticulous preparation. We recognize that our setbacks stem from inadequate preparation, and we promise to do better next time, only to repeat the same cycle. We are not very good at learning from history, much less acting on it. That's where the rule of the Red Ferrari comes in handy. Remember this rule when aiming for your event-related goals, or you might get stuck in the endless loop of "next time."

We learn from history that we do not learn from history.
Georg Hegel

When you feel a challenge is too daunting, think of Schumacher's red Ferrari or Einstein's driver. The challenge is only as tough as you make it out to be. I learned this lesson through public speaking, where it made all the difference between failing miserably and surpassing expectations.

While the three scenarios described at the beginning of the chapter may seem exaggerated, they are not far from reality. I once gave a speech completely unprepared, thinking it would be easy — just like what happened in Scenario One. I've also been terrified of public speaking, resulting in a performance worse than described in Scenario Two. On the flip side, there have been occasions where I delivered exceptional speeches. The example in Scenario Three was based on my real-life speech to a colleague named Ekaterina, almost verbatim. Before that speech, Ekaterina had vowed never to return, yet she was back in less than six months. Just a formality, huh?

***

The Rule of the Red Ferrari:

Take control through rehearsal. This is how you can bring your A-game and outperform the "Red Ferrari effect."

Chapter 5

Borrow from Tomorrow?

The tragedy in life doesn't lie in not reaching your goal. The tragedy lies in having no goal to reach.

Benjamin E. Mays

The Ten-Year Wait

You've probably heard the old Soviet-era joke about how long everything took — especially getting a car. After years of saving, a man finally places his order. The dealer hands him the receipt and says, "Come back in ten years to pick it up."

"Morning or afternoon?" the buyer asks.

The dealer raises an eyebrow. "It's ten years from now. What difference does it make?"

The man lets out a sigh. "The plumber's coming in the morning."

***

Three Tales of Triumph and Tragedy

How Living for Today Can Ruin Your Tomorrow

In this chapter, we're diving into another crucial piece of the success puzzle. But just like before, I'm not going to hand it to you — you'll get the chance to discover it for yourself. More fun that way, isn't it?

Let's kick things off with some gripping true stories from the high-stakes world of mind sports. We'll follow the lives of three brilliant minds who chased the thrill of the game to dangerous extremes — and paid the ultimate price. Their tales are marked by staggering success and sudden, catastrophic collapse. Fortunes were found and lost, empires built and crumbled, and moments of fleeting euphoria dissolved into deep existential struggle. Ready to dive in?

The Magician Who Played with Fire

Mikhail Tal's Rise and Fall

Mikhail Tal, a Latvian-born chess prodigy, took the chess world by storm at just 22. In 1959, at the Candidates Tournament in Yugoslavia, he delivered a masterclass in dominance, scoring an astonishing 20 out of 28 points. This monumental victory earned him the right to challenge the reigning world champion, Mikhail Botvinnik. The following year, Tal crushed Botvinnik in their match and became the youngest chess world champion in history at 23. He was young, charismatic, had a captivating playing style, and was a World Champion. Everything seemed destined for a life of happiness and success.

But it wasn't going to be.

Tal lived for the moment, as if tomorrow didn't exist. Partying, drinking, and smoking seemed more urgent than defending his title. Inevitably, his health began to falter in his twenties, and lacking the physical stamina required, he lost his world championship title back to Botvinnik.

His self-destructive lifestyle continued to take its toll. By the age of 32, his kidney had to be removed, a stark warning of the price he was paying. But Tal didn't slow down. By 1992, his life had withered away as visibly as his health. At the annual Moscow Blitz Chess Tournament, he lay gravely ill, barely clinging to life in a hospital bed. But chess was in his veins, and he wasn't going to miss it. Defying logic (and medical orders) he escaped from the hospital to play in the tournament he loved the most. Frail and gaunt, a shadow of the vibrant genius he once was, he sat across from none other than Garry Kasparov, the reigning world champion.

What happened next became the stuff of legend.

Playing with his signature aggressive style, Tal sacrificed a piece to stir up complications. It was the kind of audacious move only Tal would dare attempt. Kasparov, one of the greatest minds chess has ever known, couldn't crack the puzzle. After a monumental struggle, Kasparov ran out of time. It was the only game Kasparov lost in that entire tournament – to a man who had literally escaped his deathbed.

One month later, Mikhail Tal died at the age of 55, his body worn down by decades of reckless abandon. Once hailed as the most charismatic world champion in history, he left behind a legacy of brilliance and tragedy.

The Genius Who Gambled It All Away

Stu Ungar's Story of Talent and Turmoil

Stu Ungar is a name whispered with reverence in the world of card games. He wasn't just a player – he was a force of nature. As a young man, he rose to prominence as one of the greatest gin rummy players in history. His most famous match came against Harry Stein, who was then regarded as the world's best player. The stakes were high, but Ungar didn't just win – he annihilated him, taking 86 straight games without losing a single one. From that moment, Ungar's status as the undisputed champion of gin rummy was set in stone.

But gin wasn't big enough for him.

In 1980, Ungar set his sights on poker, and it took him only two tournaments to become world champion. In the final match, he beat Doyle Brunson, one of poker's all-time greats. The following year, he defended his title, cementing his place as the best in the world.

At 28, Stu Ungar was on top of the world. He was the best gin player on the planet, one of the most feared No Limit Hold'em players in history, and a multi-millionaire with a beautiful wife and two adoring children. Everything seemed destined for a life of happiness and success.

But it wasn't going to be.

Ungar's passion for action was just as intense as Tal's, if not more so. He was an adrenaline junkie, driven not by money but by the thrill of putting everything on the line. Unfortunately, this desire for excitement led him down a dangerous path, ultimately leading to drug addiction in search of even more intense experiences. He squandered most of his money on reckless gambling. The rest he spent on cocaine. In a few short years, his life went from dream to nightmare.

By the early 1990s, Stu Ungar had lost almost everything. His marriage had ended in divorce, his son tragically took his own life, and his finances were in shambles from gambling and drugs. The 1990 World Championships perfectly captured his life at the time. He dominated the first two days, amassing a huge chip lead, but failed to show up for the third day. He was later found unconscious in his hotel room due to a drug overdose. Even while lying in the hospital, his stack managed to hold onto a spot in the top ten before being eroded by blinds and antes.

The final chapter of Ungar's life, spanning 1997-1998, showcased both his brilliance and his downfall. He desperately tried to play in the 1997 World Championships. He stayed awake for 24 hours straight before the tournament, trying to borrow money to enter. In the last seconds, he was given the money he needed. The first day was shaky for him as he battled sleepiness, but by the second day, he had rediscovered his old magic, crushing opponents with his usual ultra-aggressive style. Once again, he had a huge chip lead going into the final day, but this time he didn't squander it, winning the title convincingly. 17 years after his first title, Stu Ungar became the second player (after John Moss) to win the most prestigious title in poker three times. It was his last world championship, winning in both his first and last appearances.

The following year, Stu Ungar withdrew from the tournament just minutes before it started. Constant drug abuse had made him unfit to play. Later, in an interview, he admitted regretting his decision not to play in the event he loved most:

"I realized how wrong I was not to show up. I really want to win another world championship. I want to win a fourth world championship because nobody has done that before. That would really separate me from the rest of them. And I guarantee I will win another championship – if I'm alive."

At the time of the next world championships, Stu Ungar was no longer alive. He died at the age of 45, his life cut short by years of drug abuse. His unique talent and tragic demise tell a story of remarkable success tarnished by addiction. Despite winning over 30 million dollars playing poker, Stu Ungar left this world with nothing to his name but a legacy marred by addiction and unfulfilled dreams.

The Gambler Who Turned $50 into $40 Million – Then Lost It All

The Legend of Archie Karas

In December 1992, Archie Karas arrived in Las Vegas with just $50 in his pocket. By the time he left, he'd amassed over $40 million. What happened in between is known in gambling folklore as "The Run" – the most legendary winning streak in gambling history.

It began with pool. Karas hustled pool sharks until no one would play him. Then he moved to poker, where he faced off against some of the biggest names in history: Doyle Brunson, Chip Reese, Johnny Moss, Johnny Chan, and even Stu Ungar. One by one, they tried, and one by one, they fell. None could stop him.

By 1995, Archie Karas had achieved what most of us can only dream of. He was a multimillionaire, a world-famous shark in both pool and poker, and the man behind a legendary winning streak that would go down in gambling history. Everything seemed destined for a life of happiness and success.

You probably already suspect that it wasn't going to be.

> *Money means nothing to me.... The things I want, money can't buy: health, freedom, love, happiness.*
>
> **Archie Karas**

Instead of cashing out or banking his winnings, Karas did the opposite. He sought action. He continued to risk everything he had won, and he wasn't smart about it. He played dice, baccarat, and other rubbish with negative odds. Within weeks, he lost most of his money, and within a year, he was broke.

The reasons for his downfall are clear. Just like Mikhail Tal and Stu Ungar, he was crazy for action. He needed excitement like water and was willing to sacrifice odds if necessary.

"I don't care about money, so I have no fear. I don't care if I lose it," he once said. A classic example of sacrificing future assets for present-day excitement.

Years later, Archie Karas returned to gambling, but his desperation for action had grown reckless. In 2013, he was arrested for marking blackjack cards at a casino. This wasn't just a bad bet – it was cheating. He was convicted and sentenced to three years of probation.

Once hailed as the man who turned $50 into $40 million, Archie Karas is now remembered as the man who had it all – and lost it all. Unlike Mikhail Tal and Stu Ungar, he survived his relentless hunger for excitement – but it cost him everything else.

***

The Cost of Borrowing from Tomorrow

What These Stories Teach Us About Success

These were three stories of geniuses who, by borrowing excitement from the future, ultimately destroyed their lives. So, what lessons can we learn from these stories? They are extreme examples, but going to extremes makes it easier to see the truth.

What all three of these people had in common was a complete failure to see ahead, to imagine where they wanted to be five or ten years later. Of course, it's impossible to predict the future, but at least we shouldn't live as if there is none.

It's time to introduce the next ingredient in the success formula: establishing a long-term goal. This means visualizing who you aspire to be and what you aim to achieve in the years to come.

Why is it essential to have a broader perspective on your life? No, I don't want to discourage you from drugs, drinking, and gambling if that's what you're thinking based on these stories. First, you're not reading a manual for becoming a saint. And second, I hope you don't need this book to avoid going overboard with those three sins. Not borrowing today's fun from tomorrow at the cost of your health or wealth is too obvious to spend more time on than we already have with these stories. This book is all about tips and tricks, not moral lectures.

There are other reasons why having a long-term goal is an important ingredient in the success formula, like dealing with tough times, failures, and bad luck. Giving up is the easy way out, but nobody has ever won anything by quitting. Let's look at an example to illustrate the effect of having a long-term goal.

The Tale of the Piano Player

How Long-Term Goals Help You Handle Short-Term Losses

Imagine you want to become a piano player. You take a few lessons from experts and buy a piano so you can practice at home. Then you take even more lessons and practice every evening. If you're dedicated enough to put in the effort and practice regularly and frequently, you'll become good at playing the piano – if your neighbors don't kill you first.

It wouldn't be long before you start planning your very first unofficial concert. Probably nothing big — just a small event for friends and family, and maybe some other piano enthusiasts who started their journey with you (definitely not your neighbors, though).

Now imagine time flies by and you have the concert … and it goes horribly wrong. You're nervous, feel like you've forgotten everything you've learned, and fail miserably.

Picture yourself in that moment. The concert is over, and despite your subpar performance, everyone is still applauding. Maybe out of sympathy or because they're not musically inclined and didn't notice anything going wrong (this would definitely be the case with me — I have no ear for music whatsoever, and unless you literally destroyed your piano, I'd probably think you just played a masterpiece).

But the applause isn't helping. The audience (and definitely me) might not realize it, but YOU KNOW it was bad. You know it the next day and the day after that. It reminds you every time you see the piano in the corner of your living room. What would you do?

It's easy to get frustrated or even depressed when things go wrong. It can seriously harm your enthusiasm for a career as a piano player. You might even give up and sell your piano at the first opportunity. While this might be the best thing ever for your neighbors, it's not the optimal choice for you.

Now, imagine having a long-term plan in place. Let's say there's a piano competition eleven months from now, something like a local "Got Talent" show, but only for piano players. Your goal is to participate and win (or at least make a good impression if you're not overly ambitious). Whether it's sensible to participate in a "Got Talent" show is another question, but it does give you a broader perspective on your life (or at least your piano career).

Having this plan makes facing the aftermath of a lackluster performance much easier. You realize that beyond personal judgment, there are no real consequences. Your loved ones still support you. Remember, they even applauded after your performance (if one of your friends happens to be me, I'd still genuinely believe you're a great piano player). While your neighbors might not be fans, their dislike predates your recent blunder. Their primary concern is for you to stop playing, regardless of your skill level. So, the only real consequence of the failed concert is your own perception. Placing too much emphasis on this performance could lead to unnecessary turmoil. But if you see it as the first step towards achieving your goal of winning the talent competition, it allows you to gain perspective. You realize the critical event is nearly a year away, making this setback just a valuable lesson learned. You don't get frustrated but continue, even stronger than before.

The Power of the Long Game

Why Patience Pays Off

Think back to my Quoridor experiment. The first ten games I played mirror your disastrous piano performance. Despite losing continuously, I persisted because of my long-term aspiration – to win the Quoridor tournament at the Pentamind World Championships. When you have long-term goals, you don't see difficulty in every opportunity; you see an opportunity in every difficulty.

> *All men who have achieved great things have been great dreamers.*
>
> **Orison Swett Marden**

I consistently rely on the idea of long-term goals in my life. In mind sports, I adopt a one-year perspective, shifting my focus from one World Championship to the next. The ultimate goal is always the "Worlds," and every competition leading up to it serves as vital preparation for the grand finale. When I face defeat at a national championship or a smaller tournament, I refuse to let despair consume me. Instead, I see it as valuable feedback on my current standing and an indicator of where I need to focus my improvement efforts.

In areas outside of mind sports, my goals often extend further into the future. Pursuing a PhD, for instance, is a long-term goal by its very nature, typically requiring four to eight years to complete. It's unthinkable to write a doctoral thesis in less than a year unless you're a genius superhuman. Those who have delved into the realm of scientific research understand the frustrations that accompany writing papers. The process demands significant time and energy, from managing references to navigating the peer-review process. It's not uncommon for your paper to be rejected after all that effort, adding to the exasperation.

However, having a long-term goal like obtaining a PhD provides a framework for handling these setbacks. Recognizing that a single paper's rejection holds little significance in the grand scheme of things helps mitigate disappointment. Your PhD thesis is still very much on the agenda; nothing is lost in that regard. Embracing this perspective allows for resilience in the face of setbacks, enabling you to stay on course toward your goals.

I've shared this rule with several friends who have come up with some creative solutions. One friend, Michael, set himself a long-term goal of living to a hundred years. At 35 years old, he had a 65-year goal ahead of him. His short-term goals were primarily focused on his accounting work, so I doubted the effectiveness of aiming to challenge the world record of Methuselah, as it seemed unrelated. I thought that if you make mistakes during a crucial presentation, leading to doubts about your competence, striving to outlive your friends and relatives wouldn't ease your frustration. But surprisingly, it worked for Michael. He once had a disastrous meeting with the CEO, but his long-term goal helped him handle the disappointment better. He immediately chose a healthy meal after the meeting, balancing the negative emotions with positive ones from eating healthily. Maximizing his life expectancy was more important to him than impressing management.

Michael's story challenged my belief that long-term goals needed to align closely with short-term goals to help us cope with failure. His example showed that unrelated goals can also work. Pursuing a long and healthy life is a valuable goal overall, so I recommend everyone consider it. Even better is to phrase it as "Maximizing your chances for a long and healthy life." This way, if you get hit by lightning and die unexpectedly, you can have no regrets and can proudly claim you achieved your goal.

Nevertheless, it's still beneficial to have long-term goals that relate to short-term ones. While almost any significant long-term goal can help in handling failures, it's also essential not to abandon current projects unnecessarily. For instance, if you're a junior accountant and you fail your first task, the desire to live healthily may not motivate you to persist in your accounting career, but striving to become a respected accountant might.

Having a long-term goal is a key strategy for managing setbacks and staying on track. It's important to recognize that failure is a natural part of life and it happens often. We all have numerous short-term goals in various aspects of our lives, and it's unrealistic to expect we won't encounter failures along the way. The key is not to be disheartened by these setbacks but to view them as learning opportunities.

Renowned English economist John Maynard Keynes famously declared, "In the long run, we are all dead." However, this statement does not negate the importance of setting long-term goals. Our goals can even take our entire lives to achieve, such as minimizing our ecological impact or aiming to live for a century, as my friend Michael aspires to do (he's off to a good start so far). While it is true that eventually, we all meet the same fate, having goals that extend into the future can provide us with direction and purpose, aiding us in navigating the challenges of the present.

The Rule of Long-Term Goals:

Have in mind what you want to accomplish in one to ten years from now. Anchor your goals to the future. Don't borrow from tomorrow.

Why does it work? Recognizing the existence of tomorrow prevents making foolish choices today. Long-term goals serve as a source of resilience, preventing premature quitting in the face of minor setbacks.

Just like the rule of talent, the rule of long-term goals also serves to sustain your motivation during challenging times. While the talent trap may bring you down before you have even had a chance to fail properly, having a long-term goal helps you to keep your head up after a failure.

What If You Run Out of Time?

When Long-Term Goals Don't Go As Planned

The chapter wouldn't be complete without addressing a critical question: What happens if time runs out and the long-term goal isn't realized? Picture this scenario: the highly anticipated Got Piano Talent competition day has finally arrived, but you fall short. Or perhaps I am unable to clinch victory at the World Championships. Maybe you face expulsion before obtaining your scientific degree.

Long-term goals are a valuable tool for warding off frustration and maintaining focus after failing to achieve short-term goals. It's not solely about reaching the set objectives, but rather about preserving motivation and positivity in the face of adversity. Therefore, the mere presence of long-term goals holds intrinsic value, regardless of whether they are attained.

Furthermore, the beauty lies in the fact that new goals can be established promptly. The opportunity to set fresh goals is always present. Whether it involves taking another shot at a piano talent competition or aiming for redemption at the annual Pentamind World Championships, the possibility for a fresh start is always within reach. While securing another PhD opportunity may present a greater challenge, there are always alternate aspirations to pursue. You might also consider having multiple long-term objectives simultaneously, ensuring a continuous flow of goals to work toward, even if one falls short.

Additionally, goals don't have to be solely quantifiable. Instead of fixating on winning the piano talent hunt, aim to position yourself for success. This shift in perspective mirrors my approach to the World Championships: winning may not always be within my control, but putting forth my best effort certainly is. Such adaptable goals are easier to attain, as achieving them doesn't hinge solely on victory. Even in defeat, success can still be found in giving it your all.

Jane's journey

Let's once more revisit my developer friend Jane and her desire to become a data scientist. We've discussed her journey in light of the first four rules in previous chapters. Let's assume she's got them all right and explore the rule of long-term goals.

In the previous chapter, Jane was preparing for a job interview, and our advice was for her to rehearse extensively. However, success is never guaranteed, no matter how well-prepared one is. Unexpected things can happen, and even if Jane does everything right, there's still a possibility she may be deemed unsuitable for the position by the interviewers. Such an outcome can be disheartening after dedicating considerable time and effort. Jane might find herself frustrated and disappointed, tempted to distance herself from a pursuit that has primarily evoked negative feelings.

To prevent this scenario, Jane must keep her long-term goal in mind. The job interview and its associated test task are just short-term, event-related goals that don't dictate her future. Her ultimate aim is to become a data scientist, and not being selected for the team at the first opportunity should not deter her from pursuing this ambition. The long-term goal remains achievable, and maintaining this perspective will help Jane cope with any setbacks during the interview process. Instead of letting failures discourage her, Jane can use them as learning experiences that will ultimately propel her toward her desired career path.

***

A Russian Perspective on Perseverance

What Russians Teach Us About Enduring Hardship

Embracing a long-term perspective can greatly aid people in dealing with difficult circumstances. Have you ever pondered the reasons behind the positive mindset displayed by many Russians, along with their unwavering support for their leaders, even in the face of extreme challenges? Despite widespread poverty and political turmoil in Russia, one might expect citizens to feel discontent. So, what fuels this positivity and hospitality? It seems that having something to look forward to in the future makes enduring hardship easier.

Remember the story of the Russian man who waited a decade to receive the car he had paid for in advance? In a country where delays and obstacles are commonplace, having long-term goals becomes almost inevitable. It's a coping mechanism, a metaphorical light at the end of a dark tunnel. While today may bring only meager sustenance, like potato peels, the promise of a car in ten years brings hope and motivation.

Another aspect of this long-term perspective involves the aspiration for Russia to regain its former glory, expand its reach, and reclaim its status as a global powerhouse. This grand vision acts as a source of inspiration, propelling people through the toughest of times. The significance of having a long-term goal cannot be overstated, especially amid adversity. It is the collective dream of a better tomorrow that energizes the Russian people, allowing them to persevere through present challenges.

In conclusion, having a long-term goal is a strategic tool that empowers you to persevere after failing your short-term goals. It serves as a guiding light to navigate setbacks and misfortunes, offering a beacon of hope even in the darkest times. Additionally, a long-term goal can reignite your sense of purpose when it fades, stopping you from sacrificing future well-being for immediate gratification. Had fallen geniuses Mikhail Tal, Stu Ungar, and Archie Karas understood the power of long-term goals, their life stories might have taken a drastically different turn.

***

The Rule of Long-Term Goals:

Have in mind what you want to accomplish in one to ten years from now. Anchor your goals to the future. Don't borrow from tomorrow.

Chapter 6

Nobody Else Has a Clue Either

Two things are infinite: the universe and human stupidity, and I'm not sure about the universe.

Albert Einstein

The Hero of the Plane

When the pilot passed out, panic erupted in the cabin. Nobody knew what to do. Anxious passengers looked around, hoping someone would step forward — but nobody did. Everyone just stared at each other, waiting for the "expert" to take charge. Nobody moved — except one man. He stepped forward, grabbed the radio, and said the words you'd expect from a professional:

"This is passenger 12B. I have no idea how to fly this plane, but I'm ready to try."

He followed instructions from air traffic control, took control of the plane, and, after a nerve-wracking descent, successfully landed it on the runway.

Later, the media hailed him as a hero. But when asked how he found the courage to step forward, he gave a simple answer:

"Nobody else was doing anything. So I figured I might as well try."

The biggest mistake people make isn't being clueless. It's assuming that everyone else has a clue.

***

Succeeding While Hardly Having a Clue

Given that we spend a significant portion of our lives at work, our career success plays a crucial role in shaping our overall satisfaction with life. Chapters 6, 7, and 8 focus on practical strategies and dispelling myths to elevate your workplace performance. This chapter examines the significance of specialized knowledge and skills, which can be cultivated through learning and consistently applied in your professional pursuits. To illustrate a critical misunderstanding, I'll share some insights from my own career outside the realm of mind sports.

Though pursuing a PhD isn't strictly a job, let's start there. It may sound surprising, but the contrast between my perceived and actual competence in science is vast. I lack any real interest in the subject, which has made every scientific article I've written a laborious battle against the odds. Nevertheless, to my amazement, each of my papers managed to secure publication in my preferred journals – an achievement that some of my more ambitious colleagues struggled to attain, often facing numerous rejections.

In hindsight, pursuing a field I lacked curiosity in was probably not the wisest choice. I hadn't yet understood the rule of curiosity back then and therefore I made a poor decision. I would surely have done better following my curiosity but it's too late to whine about my stupid career decisions now, so let's return to my academic misadventures.

Once I completed my three required papers, it was time for the pièce de résistance – my PhD thesis. As you might expect, given my utter indifference toward scientific inquiry, my thesis was not much better than my lackluster papers. I didn't understand half of what I was doing and was probably misinterpreting the other half. In the end, my thesis was a Potemkin village – grand on the outside, hollow on the inside. Nevertheless, I walked away with my PhD.

When I later transitioned into the corporate world as a data science "expert," I felt like an imposter. I was convinced my colleagues were light-years ahead of me, and any moment my cover would be blown. But as time passed, I realized something shocking: *They didn't have a clue either.* The field-specific buzzwords that had initially made them sound like ultra-smart superhumans were essentially all they knew. I was no longer worse than my colleagues.

Later, as a manager, I once again felt inadequate. I had no formal training in management (apart from a short course) and zero prior experience. Yet, astonishingly, my Risk team became the top-performing department in the company — and the only one without internal conflicts. I had convinced myself I was a terrible manager, but reality showed me I was no worse than anyone else.

This overview of my career reveals a singular pattern: no matter what I undertake, I often feel mediocre at best. I assumed that many of my colleagues were far more competent than me. But as time went on, I began to wonder: *Do they feel the same way?*

The "Everybody Else Is Smarter" Fallacy

> *The best advice I've ever received is no-one else knows what they are doing either.*
>
> **Ricky Gervais**

Years ago, I shared my theory with a few coworkers — an accountant, a lawyer, an SEO specialist, and a recruiter. I proposed that while they likely felt overwhelmed by my field of risk management, they probably assumed I could competently perform their jobs. They all agreed with my hypothesis.

The accountant admitted that with just a few months of intensive training, nearly anyone could manage her responsibilities. The lawyer admitted to relying on Google and referencing legal statutes — something any of us could do with some practice. The SEO specialist said that SEO strategy seemed like rocket science at first, but ultimately boiled down to simple rules anyone could learn.

When the recruiter remained silent for a few moments, we eagerly waited for her take. After all, she had achieved great results and was viewed by most as a great expert in the field of recruiting. What she finally said was this:

"I never actually learned how to be a recruiter. I joined as an office manager and only temporarily moved to recruiting when the previous recruiter went on maternity leave."

There it was. The truth. Nobody had a clue either.

While the perception of some of our colleagues being "genius-level" smart is prevalent, it is frequently misguided. It emerges from our awareness of others' unique knowledge and expertise. But here's the truth: Most "experts" are barely ahead of you, and many aren't ahead at all.

When it comes to specialized knowledge in your field, you and your colleagues might each know something that the others don't. But these differences tend to cancel each other out, and all in all, you're all approximately on the same level. But the key here is that this expertise level is not very high. I was hopeless in the realm of science yet found myself surpassing many of my peers in understanding. My doctoral thesis, which now serves as oven kindling, is not alone in its lackluster impact — numerous academic papers seem to disrespect trees by existing in print form. I fully expected my limited knowledge of data science to become quickly apparent, but instead, I was hailed as an expert in the field. We have to stop deluding ourselves into believing that we are surrounded by mind-bending geniuses. If those exist, they don't share the office with us.

The secret to success is recognizing that everyone else is winging it too. If you're still hesitant, consider this: The world is not run by geniuses, experts, or prodigies. It's run by people who have no clue what they're doing — but they act anyway.

The Rule of Stupidity:

Success isn't miles away — it's just one small, confident step ahead. Everyone is winging it. You don't need to have all the answers to take action and win.

Why does it work? Viewing the path to success as an insurmountable mountain can be incredibly demotivating. By shifting your perspective and eliminating this mental barrier, you can stay motivated and focused on your goals.

The Rule of Stupidity teaches us that most people are operating at a basic level, and that small, consistent actions can easily set you apart.

Why "Experts" Appear So Smart

If it's true that most people only possess basic-level knowledge in their roles, then why do some of our colleagues seem genuinely brilliant? The answer lies in relative perception.

To illustrate, imagine you're asked to rate a co-worker's expertise. If your own knowledge of their field is close to zero, then even if their skill is a 5 out of 100, it feels like they're infinitely more knowledgeable than you. A 5 out of 100 feels like a genius next to a 0.

But here's the twist: if you had a knowledge level of 4 (instead of 0), that same person wouldn't feel like a genius anymore. Their "advantage" would seem tiny. If you've ever learned a new language, you know how this works. At first, anyone fluent sounds like a wizard. But as you learn more, you start to realize, "Hey, they're not a wizard. They just know 50 more words than I do."

This is the essence of why "experts" appear so smart. It's an illusion. It's not their absolute knowledge that matters — it's the gap between you and them.

Here's the truth: Most of the people you view as "super smart" are only marginally ahead of you. The distance isn't as vast as it seems. They have a few extra bits of knowledge, a few extra moves up their sleeve, but that's it. They're not light-years ahead. They're one or two moves ahead.

Closing the Knowledge Gap: The Power of Small Wins

Everybody is stupid in almost everything.

Author

The Rule of Stupidity reminds us that small, consistent actions are enough to surpass the majority of people who are operating at a basic level. Let's see how this works in practice.

If everyone is working with only surface-level knowledge, it means the knowledge gap between you and them is remarkably small. And here's the kicker: that small gap is the only thing standing between you and a significant competitive advantage.

One of the most effective ways to close the knowledge gap is through the principle of "small wins." Every time you learn a new concept, master a new tool, or acquire a useful trick, you move closer to the so-called "expert level." Each small win builds momentum, reinforcing the belief that you can bridge the gap.

Here's something most people don't realize: mastery isn't about monumental leaps. It's about consistent, incremental progress. No one wakes up one day and becomes a master chess player, a world champion, or a data scientist. But by acquiring small pieces of knowledge over time, you inevitably surpass your peers.

This is where the rule of stupidity becomes a superpower. If everyone around you is playing at a basic level, then every small advantage you acquire moves you closer to the top of the leaderboard. When you recognize that "most people are guessing their way through," you'll stop viewing the gap as insurmountable and start seeing it as conquerable.

Recognizing that nobody else has a clue is liberating, but what do you do with that insight? Here's how to turn it into action.

How to Act on This Insight

1. Act With Confidence (Even When You're Unsure)

Most of your colleagues are guessing too, but the difference is that "heroes" take action, while others hesitate.

What to Do:

- The next time you're in a meeting and hear an idea that sounds "off," speak up. You'll be amazed how often others nod in agreement and thank you for saying what they were thinking.
- If there is a regular meeting that feels pointless, say it. Everybody else thinks so too, but in the fear of others finding it useful, they are afraid to speak up. Speak up before everybody else and be the hero.

Example: You're in a strategy meeting, and someone proposes an idea that sounds questionable. Everyone else stays quiet. In that moment, remember: *They probably have doubts too, but they're afraid to speak up*. Be the one to say, "I have some concerns about that approach." This single moment of courage could earn you a reputation as a bold thinker.

2. Ask the "Dumb" Questions

If something doesn't make sense, ask. You'll often find that nobody else understands it either.

The fear of looking stupid stops most people from asking simple questions. Ironically, those "simple" questions often uncover the biggest mistakes. Since most people are operating at a basic level of knowledge, there's a good chance your "dumb" question isn't so dumb after all – it's something everyone else wants to ask but is too afraid to do so.

What to Do:

- Adopt a mindset that assumes other people also don't understand everything, because they don't.
- In meetings or training sessions, if something is unclear, ask for clarification immediately.
- Rephrase your questions to sound more collaborative: "Just to make sure I understand correctly..." or "I'm curious, could you explain why we're doing it this way?"

Example: Imagine you're in a meeting about a new project management tool, and someone explains a process that sounds overly complicated. You could sit in silence like everyone else, pretending you understand. *Or* you could ask, "I'm not sure I fully get that. Can you walk us through it step-by-step?" If you're thinking it, others are too, and your question will make everyone grateful you spoke up.

3. Share What You Know (Even If It Feels Basic)
You may think you have nothing valuable to teach, but you'd be wrong. Remember, most people know only the bare minimum to get by. What's "basic" for you might be groundbreaking for someone else. Teaching others also reinforces your knowledge and solidifies your reputation as a skilled, helpful person.

What to Do:

- Volunteer to explain processes to new employees. It may feel "too basic" to you, but for them, it's a lifeline.
- Share useful tips and shortcuts with your colleagues, no matter how simple they seem.

- Write "cheat sheets" or mini-guides for your team. What feels obvious to you might be revolutionary for them.

Example: At one of my previous jobs, I shared a quick, 5-minute tutorial on Excel keyboard shortcuts with my team. I thought it was basic stuff, but my manager called it "life-changing" and forwarded it to the whole department. This simple move earned me recognition as a "helpful resource" — not because I was an Excel wizard, but because I shared knowledge that everybody else felt too basic to share.

4. Drop Perfectionism — Done Is Better Than Perfect

> *Perfectionism is fear in disguise. Ship it, launch it, move forward — you can polish later.*
>
> **Author**

Perfectionism is a productivity killer. Most of the people you admire for their success aren't perfectionists. They understand the power of iteration — you make something, ship it, and improve it later. Perfectionism isn't about being "better" — it's just fear in disguise.

What to Do:

- Start before you feel ready. Done is better than perfect — get the first version done, test and refine it on the go.
- Set a deadline for completing the first version of a project. If it's a presentation, aim to finish it in one day, knowing you can edit it later.

Example: My biologist friend shared an amusing story about how she unwittingly earned the nickname "machine-whisperer." When a cutting-edge blood-testing machine for birds was introduced in their lab, her colleagues hesitated, uncertain of how to handle it. My friend, however, enthusiastically embraced the challenge. Before long, she became the department's unofficial expert on the machine, and it became policy for all blood tests to be conducted by her due to her unmatched skill with it.

When I asked about her top-notch proficiency with the machine, she simply shrugged and casually responded, "Well, I read the instructions."

The point of the story is she started using the machine before she felt "perfectly" prepared – she only had read the instructions. She knew she could learn the intricacies later. Yet, she was viewed as a true expert. Perfect? Who cares?

5. Leverage the "Everyone Is Clueless" Insight

Finally, remember the key lesson: *nobody else has a clue either.* When you internalize this fact, something magical happens – you stop overestimating others and underestimating yourself. You realize that everyone around you is just as confused as you are. But there's a difference between confused people who freeze and confused people who move. Be the one who moves.

What to Do:

- Stop putting people on pedestals. The "genius" in your department? They're just as lost as you are.
- Apply for that job you think you're "unqualified" for. The "perfect" candidates on LinkedIn are exaggerating too.
- Make a list of your biggest self-doubts, and next to each one, write down how others around you might have the exact same doubt.

Example: When I started my job in data science, I was certain my colleagues were "ultra-smart superhumans." But as I listened to their conversations, I realized that most of them didn't know the answers either. They just used fancy language to disguise it. This realization gave me the confidence to speak up, propose ideas, and even challenge their logic. Over time, I went from feeling like a rookie to being seen as a leader. The only difference? I stopped underestimating myself and stopped overestimating them.

Jane's Journey from Hesitation to Expertise

Let's join our developer friend Jane's journey again, this time looking at the scenario where she managed to turn her initial doubts around and properly use all the rules discussed so far, with the emphasis on the rule of stupidity.

When Jane first considered transitioning from her role as a developer to becoming a data scientist, she felt overwhelmed. The world of data science seemed vast and daunting. Terms like "machine learning algorithms," "big data," and "predictive analytics" felt like an entirely different language, one she was certain she could never master.

Her initial excitement was quickly overshadowed by self-doubt. She browsed job postings and LinkedIn profiles of established data scientists, only to feel like she was leagues behind. Many of them boasted impressive credentials – advanced degrees, years of experience, and certifications from prestigious institutions. Jane couldn't help but think, *What chance do I have?*

But deep down, she couldn't ignore her curiosity. She had always been fascinated by how data could unlock patterns and tell stories. One day, after yet another wave of self-doubt, she decided to take a small step. Instead of worrying about the entire mountain of knowledge she thought she needed, she started with a single, achievable goal: spend one evening learning the basics of Python.

To her surprise, the tutorial wasn't as intimidating as she'd expected. By the end of the evening, she had written her first simple program. It was nothing groundbreaking – just a script that calculated the average of a list of numbers – but it felt like magic. Jane realized she didn't need to understand everything at once. She just needed to focus on the next small step.

Encouraged, she set another micro-goal: learn how to manipulate data using Python libraries like Pandas and NumPy. Within a week, she was organizing datasets and creating basic visualizations. A month later, she was running her first simple regression analysis. Every small win built her confidence and momentum. The technical jargon that once felt alien began to make sense.

Her colleagues started to notice. During meetings, Jane began chiming in with data-driven insights. Though she still didn't consider herself a data scientist, her contributions were undeniably valuable. One day, her manager approached her with a surprising request:

"We're launching a new project that relies heavily on data analysis. Would you be interested in leading the effort?"

Jane hesitated. She wanted to say yes, but the old doubts crept back in. *Am I ready for this? What if I mess up?* But then she remembered something important: most of her colleagues were figuring things out as they went too. Nobody knew everything. The difference between success and mediocrity wasn't expertise – it was action. So, she said yes.

The project was a success. Jane's small, consistent efforts had paid off. By the time she finished, she was no longer "dabbling" in data science. She was doing it. Her confidence grew, and so did her skills. Within a year, Jane transitioned to a full-time data scientist role – a position she once thought was far beyond her reach.

Jane's journey wasn't about giant leaps or monumental breakthroughs. It was about small wins, incremental progress, and the courage to act despite uncertainty. She discovered that the gap between "beginner" and "expert" was smaller than she'd imagined — and that closing it was as simple as taking one step at a time.

Final Thoughts: Climbing the Hill, Not the Mountain

Nobody else has a clue either — and that's your advantage. Once you internalize this fact, you'll stop thinking you need to be "super talented" to succeed. You don't. You just need to do one thing: act.

Act before you're ready. Ask questions others are afraid to ask. Help your colleagues, even if you feel unqualified. Finish your work before it's perfect. Apply for that job you don't feel "qualified" for. Take that opportunity, even if it scares you. Why?

Because nobody else has a clue either.

The difference between success and mediocrity is action. The hero of the plane did not succeed because he knew everything; he succeeded because he took action.

Stop thinking of success as an impossible mountain to climb. It's a small hill, and you just need to take the first step.

You don't need to know everything. You just need to know a little more than the person next to you — and that's not as hard as it seems.

***

The Rule of Stupidity:

Success isn't miles away — it's just one small, confident step ahead.
Everyone is winging it. You don't need to have all the answers to take action and win.

Chapter 7

There Is No Wrong Time to Make the Right Decision

There is nothing so useless as doing efficiently that which should not be done at all.

Peter Drucker

The Construction Worker's Precision Paradox

A construction worker once regaled me with a story about his coworkers unearthing human remains – the oldest ever found in the country. At first, I wasn't particularly interested. But then he mentioned the bones were a staggering 200,000 years *and four months* old, and that caught my attention.

"Wait, how can you be so precise about that?" I asked, genuinely confused.

He chuckled and replied, "The experts dated the bones at 200,000 years, but that was about four months ago."

***

The Trap of Misguided Goals

In the last chapter, we focused on field-specific skills and knowledge. Now, it's time to explore another crucial element of professional success: rational decision-making through logical thinking. This skill is essential for tackling creative tasks efficiently and making better choices in complex situations. To illustrate this point, let me share a personal anecdote from my past.

It began as a typical day at the lending company where I worked. I rolled in at 10 a.m., lingered in the kitchen for a couple of hours, and eventually settled at my desk. I was in the middle of reading sports news when suddenly, something far more urgent caught my attention. An email from the CEO marked as high importance had just arrived. The email described a crisis: one of the CEO's friends had been scammed into taking out a loan from our company. The scammers hadn't stopped there — they had also drained her bank account, leaving her in a desperate situation.

With an "urgent" email from the CEO, I contacted customer support to check for similar fraud cases. To my dismay, it turned out there were several cases of scammers exploiting our lending services to deceive clients. When I returned to my desk, I saw that our Risk Manager had already swooped in with a reply to the CEO's email. He proposed immediate action to "find the best solution" for the CEO's friend, suggesting we prioritize efforts to provide her with a "soft landing."

Let's pause for a moment and reflect on the situation: was this really the most effective course of action? To evaluate it, we need to define the broader goal.

Here are three possible goals we could have pursued in this situation:

1. Find a good solution for the CEO's friend.
2. Prevent further issuance of loans to future victims of the scam.
3. Understand the full scope of clients who had been tricked into taking out loans.

Pause for a moment, dear reader. Which of these three goals would you choose as the top priority? If you were in our shoes, what would you focus on first?

From Noise to Clarity: Finding the Real Problem

If you selected the second goal, congratulations — you're thinking like a rational decision-maker. The primary problem here isn't just the CEO's friend being scammed. It's that a group of fraudsters is actively exploiting identity theft to trick our company into issuing loans to innocent people. If this problem persists, it won't just hurt the victims – it will hurt us too. Clients drained of their money can't repay their loans, and we're left with unpaid debts and a damaged reputation.

While the third goal (understanding the scope) is useful, it's not the ultimate objective. It would give relevant information to achieve the second goal and can therefore be thought of as a sub-goal. And what about the first goal? Well, that's where things get interesting. From a rational decision-making standpoint, it holds no value. Here is why.

There were already dozens of scam victims – with more almost certainly on the way. Spending time and resources to figure out a soft landing for precisely one of them is poor decision-making. There is nothing about this customer that makes her any more privileged than the other scammed clients. Being a friend of the CEO doesn't mean she needs special treatment.

This is where the concept of *relative importance* comes into play. Put simply, not all actions matter equally. We only have so much time and attention (there is opportunity cost to everything we do), and it's crucial to focus on what truly moves the needle. In this case, helping one client (even the CEO's friend) does almost nothing to stop the flow of fraudulent loans. Our priority should be preventing new fraudulent loans, not putting out fires one victim at a time.

Escaping the Trap: How to Focus on What Matters

The same principle can be illustrated by returning to the construction worker's story at the beginning of this chapter. Remember how he mentioned that the bones were 200,000 years and four months old? Those four months, while technically accurate, are entirely irrelevant compared to 200,000 years. They are just a rounding error – noise, not signal.

The same logic applies here. The CEO's friend is the 'four months' in this story – technically relevant, but ultimately irrelevant. Compared to the larger problem of ongoing fraudulent loans, focusing on this one case is meaningless. The Risk Manager should have focused on stopping future scams – a goal with far greater impact.

So, how do you avoid falling into the same trap?

If you're struggling to identify the true goal, here's a useful mental shortcut:

1. Start with the problem. What's the actual issue you're facing?
2. Define the goal. The goal is simply a solution to the problem.

If you've identified the wrong problem, you'll chase the wrong goal. In this case, the real problem wasn't that the CEO's friend had to repay a loan she didn't ask for. The real problem was that scammers had figured out how to game the system. The goal, therefore, should have been to block fraudulent loans while continuing to approve legitimate ones.

If you fail to do this analysis, you risk spending time and resources on the wrong goal. That's exactly what happened with our Risk Manager. Instead of confronting the real issue, he focused on making one client happy – at the expense of solving the core problem.

From Goal to Action: The Role of Action Points

While the Risk Manager's plan wasn't the end goal, it could have been a useful step – if it actually helped stop the scammers.

But how do you know if an action will lead to your goal? Here's a simple framework. For any proposed action, ask yourself:

1. What sub-goal does this action aim to achieve?

2. Does achieving that sub-goal move us closer to the ultimate goal?

If the answer to question two is "no," then it's time to cross that action off the list. If the answer is "yes," then you have found a useful action point. Each action point should be essential – each sub-goal should naturally lead to the next step or directly resolve the main issue.

The effectiveness of each action point can be gauged by observing whether the chain of steps remains unbroken and whether the final goal can still be reached if certain steps are omitted. If the goal can be achieved without certain steps, those actions are unnecessary.

The Chain of Action Points

The interconnected sequence of action points and goals can be visualized in the following diagram as a progression from point A to point D, where A marks the starting point and D represents the ultimate objective. However, reaching D isn't a straight leap from A. Instead, you must first reach B, then C, before finally arriving at D.

The first action point is moving from A to B, with the specific sub-goal of reaching point B. This smaller objective is crucial because it serves as the foundation for the next step. After reaching B, the next action point is moving from B to C. This step unlocks the ability to achieve C, which then sets you up to achieve D – the ultimate goal. Each action builds on the one before it, creating a logical, step-by-step process.

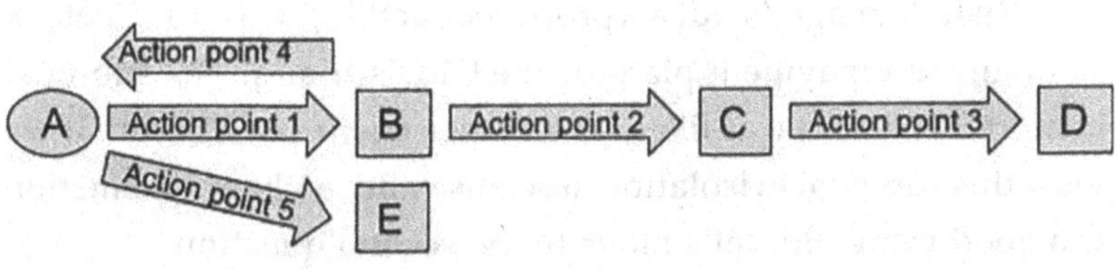

In this sequence, only three action points are required to achieve the final goal:

1. Moving from A to B (action point 1)
2. Moving from B to C (action point 2)
3. Moving from C to D (action point 3)

It's essential to recognize that any extra steps beyond what's necessary – like moving from B to A (action point 4) or from A to E (action point 5) – are counterproductive. These steps don't bring you any closer to your goal and should be avoided entirely. Each required action point has a specific purpose: either to resolve a sub-goal (like action points 1 and 2) or to achieve the final objective (like action point 3).

Another key takeaway is that only one action point should be required to achieve each sub-goal – if you're doing two things to reach the same result, one of them is probably redundant.

Identifying Wasteful Actions

Let's reconsider the Risk Manager's proposal to offer customized repayment terms for the CEO's friend. Was this a sensible action? Did it move us closer to our end goal?

We have the framework to understand whether an action will lead to our goal. Let's ask the first question:

- What sub-goal does this action aim to achieve? What is the goal behind finding a soft landing spot for the client?

The Risk Manager's idea (proposed action) was to create a customized repayment plan for the CEO's friend. The sub-goal behind this action was likely to enhance client satisfaction. If we view this sub-goal in isolation, it seems valid – client satisfaction is a good thing. But let's move to the second question:

- Does achieving this sub-goal bring us closer to the ultimate goal? Does making this one client happy get us closer to our ultimate goal of preventing scammers from exploiting our loan system?

The answer is a resounding "no." Keeping one client happy does not reduce the number of fraudulent applications. It does not protect the company from future scams. It does not prevent our clients from being scammed in the future. Therefore, this action was irrelevant — like bringing a surfboard to a ski resort.

To visualize it using the chain of action points, think of it like this: instead of moving from A to B, the Risk Manager decided to move from A to E — a pointless detour. E was never part of our original journey to D, so the move from A to E was a waste of time, effort, and resources.

Every time you're faced with a decision, keep this rule in mind: There is no greater waste than efficiently executing a task that should not be done at all. Spending time and resources on tasks that don't contribute to your goal is the ultimate form of wastefulness. This is exactly what happened here. The Risk Manager's choice to prioritize one client's happiness may have felt "helpful" at the moment, but it did nothing to solve the larger problem. His effort did not reduce fraudulent applications, did not mitigate future risks, and did not support the company's larger goal. It should not have been done at all.

> *Efficiency is doing things right. Effectiveness is doing the right things.*
>
> **Peter Drucker**

This example is a powerful reminder of why it's essential to distinguish between what's truly important and what's not. Prioritizing irrelevant details is one of the most common decision-making mistakes people make. We focus on what's directly in front of us (like the CEO's friend) instead of what actually matters (like stopping scammers).

Consider this classic example:

The Lesson of the Corrupt Politician

A corrupt politician dies and is confronted at the gates of Heaven. God appears and asks, "What have you done to deserve entry into Heaven?"

The politician replies, "A year ago, I gave 25 cents to a homeless person."

God raises an eyebrow and turns to the Archangel, who checks the official records and confirms, "He's telling the truth."

God nods. "Not bad, but a single act of generosity isn't exactly VIP status into Heaven."

"Wait, wait!" the politician interjects, "Five years ago, I also gave another 25 cents to an elderly person on the street."

The Archangel confirms the truth of this statement as well. God turns to the Archangel and asks, "What do you recommend we do with this man?"

The Archangel glances at the records and replies, "Let's give him back his 50 cents and send him to Hell."

The moral of the story is clear: small, irrelevant gestures cannot compensate for major failings. While the politician may have performed a couple of kind acts — like handing out a grand total of 50 cents to those in need — these token efforts do little to offset the weight of his more serious moral shortcomings. Those shortcomings include his corruption — and him being a politician.

Backward Induction: Solving Problems in Reverse

Now that we've established that the Risk Manager's proposal wasn't a relevant action point, the question remains: what should we have done instead? It's time to create an action plan. A strong action plan includes a clear sequence of action points, each targeting a specific sub-goal that directly contributes to the overall objective. How to create this?

One of the most effective techniques for building this action plan is called backward induction. This approach starts with the end goal — the ultimate solution to our problem — and works backward step-by-step to identify the actions and sub-goals that must be achieved along the way. By starting at the finish line and working in reverse, we ensure that every action has a clear purpose and a logical connection to the final objective. This process reveals the clearest, most efficient path to success.

Backward Induction in Action

To see backward induction in action, let's walk through our practical example. Our ultimate goal here is to reduce the number of fraudulent loan applications that we accept while still approving legitimate applications. The key challenge lies in differentiating between genuine applications and fraudulent ones.

To achieve this, we need an algorithm that can identify suspicious applications. Let's call this algorithm a fraud model. Applying this model serves as our final action point because it directly achieves our goal of rejecting fraudulent applications. The sub-goal leading up to this action is having a fully developed fraud detection model.

But how do we achieve that sub-goal? We need to build the model. Therefore, the next logical action point is clear: build the fraud detection model. This action leads to the sub-goal of having the model in place, which, in turn, allows us to apply it to our application flow and achieve the ultimate goal of preventing fraudsters from getting loans.

However, we can move further backward to identify additional action points and sub-goals. You don't build a fraud detection model out of nowhere. To create one, you need data. Specifically, you need to understand how fraudulent applications from the past differ from legitimate ones. This knowledge enables the model to recognize similar patterns in future applications. Thus, the next sub-goal becomes identifying the key differences between fraudulent and legitimate applications.

Breaking Down the Sub-Goals and Actions

How do we achieve this sub-goal? We must analyze past applications to identify patterns that separate scammers from honest clients. This analysis becomes the next action point in our chain.

But to analyze past applications, we first need to know which past applications were fraudulent and which were legitimate. We need a sample of known scammer applications and a corresponding sample of legitimate applications. This becomes another essential sub-goal.

So, how do we create this sample? We need to work with customer support and possibly law enforcement to identify applications that scammers have already submitted. This action achieves the sub-goal of creating a useful sample of scammer applications.

At this point, our backward induction chain is complete. Let's break it down step-by-step, starting from the final goal and working backward:

1. Use a predictive fraud detection model to reject fraudulent applications.
2. Build the fraud detection model using patterns that differentiate scammers from legitimate clients observed in past applications.
3. Analyze past applications to identify the differences between the samples of fraudulent and legitimate applications.
4. Create a sample of known scammer applications using data from customer support and law enforcement.

By following backward induction, we've constructed a clear, logical chain of action points. Each action point builds on the previous one, and each sub-goal directly supports the next step.

Visualizing the Process

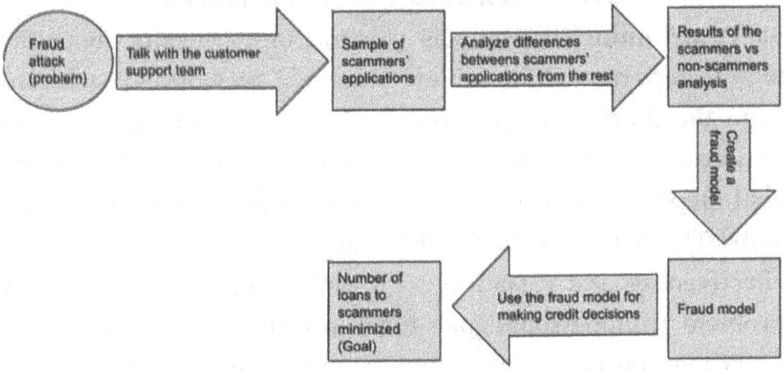

To make this even clearer, let's visualize the sequence of actions and sub-goals, starting from the beginning and moving toward the end, as shown in the figure above.

1. Start with customer support and law enforcement to identify the applications submitted by known scammers.
2. Use this information to create a sample of scammer applications, which serves as our foundation for analysis.
3. Analyze this sample to identify patterns that distinguish fraudulent applications from legitimate ones.
4. Use these patterns to build a predictive fraud detection model that can flag future fraudulent applications.
5. Incorporate the model into our credit decision process, automatically rejecting applications identified as fraudulent.

At first glance, the early steps — like gathering data from customer support — may seem unrelated to the final goal of rejecting fraudulent applications. But backward induction reveals how each step serves as a crucial building block in the chain. By following this process, we ensure that every action is meaningful, purposeful, and aligned with the larger objective.

Why Backward Induction Works

Backward induction compels you to think critically about the logical steps required to achieve your goal. By working backward from the finish line, you avoid wasting time on irrelevant or unnecessary tasks. Each action is directly connected to the end goal, step by step, ensuring no effort is wasted on detours or dead ends. The beauty of backward induction lies in its simplicity, effectiveness, and versatility — it can be applied to almost any problem, from personal goals to large-scale business challenges.

When you face a big, complex challenge, resist the urge to "just start working." Instead, begin with the end in mind and work backward. This approach makes it far easier to identify the key actions you need to take — and, just as importantly, the actions you don't.

Where the Risk Manager Went Wrong

The Risk Manager's failure stemmed from his lack of a logical decision-making process. Rather than analyzing the situation, he rushed to propose the first solution that came to mind. Unfortunately, his hasty decision failed to address the core problem. This example highlights the dangers of decision-making without proper reasoning. Taking the time to weigh the pros and cons of each option is essential to ensure that the chosen course of action addresses the root issue — not just its symptoms.

> *When making a decision of major importance, I have always found it advantageous to consider all the pros and cons.*
>
> **Sigmund Freud**

Approaching decisions methodically, with each step aligned toward resolving the problem, reduces the risk of ill-considered choices and prevents wasted effort on actions that shouldn't be done at all. The Risk Manager's predicament is not unique. Many people struggle to employ logical decision-making processes. They often make decisions reactively, without proper analysis, and the results are rarely impressive.

A more effective approach is to follow a structured framework like the one outlined earlier. This framework involves identifying the problem, establishing the goal, and using backward induction to determine the necessary action points. This step-by-step process ensures that each action serves a clear purpose. Moreover, a logical framework reduces indecision and prolonged deliberation. It's not very hard to make correct decisions; it's correct to make hard decisions.

The Rule of Decision-Making:

Start with the problem. Use backward induction to identify the action points needed to solve it. Take your time to understand what is important and what is not — because there is no greater waste than spending time and resources on something that should not be done at all.

Why does it work? Because a proper decision-making framework allows us to make better decisions. And better decisions lead to better outcomes.

> *The quality of your life is built on the quality of your decisions.*
>
> **Wesam Fawzi**

The importance of decision-making cannot be overstated. Every day, we face countless choices that shape our future. From life-changing career moves to small, everyday decisions, each one contributes to our success and happiness. Even minor choices accumulate over time, leading to significant long-term impacts. Ultimately, success is a reflection of the decisions we make.

Don't end up like the construction worker, the corrupt politician, or the hasty Risk Manager mentioned in this chapter. Each of them failed to recognize what truly mattered, succumbing to one of the most fundamental pitfalls of decision-making: focusing on the irrelevant while neglecting the essential.

***

The Rule of Decision-Making:

Start with the problem. Use backward induction to identify the action points needed to solve it. **Take your time to understand what is important and what is not — because there is no greater waste than spending time and resources on something that should not be done at all.**

Chapter 8

Answer First, Ask Later

Talent wins games, but teamwork and intelligence win championships.

Michael Jordan

The Misguided Advisor

In a prosperous kingdom, a wise king relied on a council of esteemed advisors, each celebrated for their unique expertise. Among them was the eldest advisor, a renowned expert in global trade. His years of dedicated service had earned him the king's unwavering trust. Tirelessly committed to mastering the complexities of his field, the advisor spent his days immersed in the intricacies of trade, always anticipating the king's future need for guidance.

One day, the king sought counsel on a pressing domestic policy issue. Naturally, he turned to his venerable advisor. But to the king's surprise, the advisor humbly admitted he could not offer advice. "My time is fully devoted to studying global trade," he explained, "I have not kept up with domestic affairs." The king, understanding yet disappointed, sought the wisdom of other council members instead.

This pattern repeated itself. Each time the king approached him with new questions on matters outside of trade, the advisor's response remained the same — polite but dismissive. His world was confined to trade, and he showed little interest in topics beyond it. Over time, the king's confidence in the advisor began to erode. No longer seeing him as a reliable source of counsel, the king turned to other advisors for guidance.

Then, a moment of great significance arrived. The kingdom faced a pivotal decision regarding foreign trade — a decision perfectly suited to the advisor's expertise. This was his moment to shine. But by then, the king had already grown accustomed to seeking answers elsewhere. Without hesitation, he turned to the other advisors, none of whom matched the seasoned advisor's depth of knowledge on trade. As a result, the king made a decision uninformed by the very insights that could have guided him to a better outcome.

By focusing too narrowly on his specialty and refusing to engage beyond it, the advisor left his expertise untapped at the moment it was needed most. His knowledge, vast as it was, went unnoticed — not because it lacked value, but because he failed to make it accessible.

***

Mary's Marketing Mystery

Mary, a dedicated marketing specialist at a financial technology company, stared intently at the freshly printed report in front of her. It was a comprehensive analysis she had painstakingly crafted to evaluate the profitability of various marketing channels. The report displayed key performance indicators for each channel, starting with the cost of acquiring a single paying customer, followed by conversion rates at different stages of the application process, and finally, the bad rates associated with each channel.

Drawing from this data, Mary had ingeniously fused these metrics into a single, all-encompassing measure to benchmark the effectiveness of each channel. She dubbed it *Mary's Marketing Model* — a standardized, quantitative tool that could compare performance across channels at a glance. For Mary, this was more than just a model — it was a triumph. Finally, she had a clear, objective way to assess and rank the impact of each marketing channel.

Excited by her achievement, Mary eagerly ranked the channels from best to worst, ready to present her findings to the Chief of Marketing. She felt a deep sense of pride and satisfaction — until she noticed something odd.

Her eyes narrowed as she scanned the report. Something was off. Until now, she'd focused solely on the ratios — the key focus of her performance indicator — but this time, she glanced at the total counts. Her heart sank. The total number of observations was astronomically high — far higher than it should have been. The figure strained credibility.

Doubt crept in. Mary checked the official sales report to verify the actual number of applications over the past year. Her worst fear was confirmed. The counts in her report were wildly inflated.

Her chest tightened with frustration. All the hours she had poured into devising the new indicator, writing SQL queries, and refining the methodology seemed to have been in vain. She sat back, wracking her brain. *Where did I go wrong?*

Her first instinct was to recheck the logic. Carefully, she traced her steps from the start, reviewing each part of the code, double and triple-checking for mistakes. After an hour of grueling scrutiny, she had a breakthrough.

"Why did I base the sample on the contract signing date instead of the payment date?" she muttered to herself, realizing her misstep. She reasoned that contracts without completed payments could have inflated the counts. With newfound resolve, she corrected the logic in her code, excluding unpaid contracts, and ran the query.

But nothing changed. The inflated counts remained exactly the same.

Her initial hypothesis had crumbled. Confusion swirled in her mind. Her frustration grew. *Okay, maybe I missed something.* She scoured the code again, this time with renewed focus, convinced she'd overlooked a simple typo or misplaced condition. But the logic was sound — at least on paper. Yet, the numbers stubbornly refused to budge.

Her mind bounced from one failed theory to the next. The deeper she investigated, the further away the solution seemed to drift. Each new theory felt like progress at first, but none got her closer to the truth.

Exhausted and overwhelmed, Mary glanced at her watch. It was already late in the afternoon. She had spent the entire workday chasing shadows. Realizing that her brain was on the verge of burnout, she decided to take a much-needed break and grab a cup of coffee.

Mary entered the kitchen to find it nearly empty — except for me, of course.

"Hi, Andres," she greeted me with a wry smile. "Nice to see you in the kitchen again. Every time I come in here, you're here too."

"Yup, I just had my desk moved in here," I replied with mock seriousness. "Now I can work from the kitchen full-time."

We both laughed as Mary prepared to negotiate with the coffee machine.

Just then, Jim walked in — a data analyst known for his coding skills. Mary's eyes lit up. *An opportunity.*

"Hey, Jim," she called out casually, "I'm having some issues with a report I'm working on. The numbers are off, and I think there's something wrong with the SQL logic. Would you mind taking a quick look at it?"

Jim hesitated. "I'd love to, but I'm knee-deep in deploying a new product. It's going to be a few days before I can check it out."

Mary sighed, nodding in reluctant acceptance. "No worries. Thanks anyway."

She poured her coffee and sat down, staring into the cup like it might offer her answers. Meanwhile, Jim brewed his coffee and, as he prepared to leave, he glanced over at me.

"Hey, Andres, still holding court in the kitchen, huh?" he quipped, raising his coffee in salute.

"Gotta protect my territory," I shot back, grinning. *Why does everyone comment on me being in the kitchen? I hardly even spend half the day here.*

After Jim left, I noticed Mary hadn't gone back to her desk. *This is my chance.*

"I overheard your conversation with Jim," I said cautiously. Mary glanced up, intrigued. "Want to send me the code? I can take a look."

Her eyes lit up. "Seriously? That would be amazing. I'll send it over right now."

I dove into the SQL query line by line. For an hour, I retraced Mary's logic, hoping a fresh pair of eyes would spot the issue. But it was like chasing ghosts. The code looked fine. I tried adjusting filters, double-checking joins, and even tested a few wild ideas. Nothing worked.

I felt the same confusion Mary must have felt. I stood up, stretched, and let out a sigh. *What am I missing?* Then it hit me — *Peter.*

Peter was the company's best developer, known for his knack for debugging even the trickiest problems. I made a beeline for his desk.

"Hey, Peter," I said, showing him my laptop. "Mary's working on a report, but the number of signed contracts is way too high. Any chance you could take a look?"

Peter nodded, eyes on the screen. After a moment of scanning the code, he nodded again, more firmly this time.

"The issue is with the sales table," he said. "It has duplicate IDs."

"Duplicate IDs?" I echoed, feeling like I should have known this.

"Yep," Peter confirmed. "It's a known issue, but it's not a top priority for IT, so it hasn't been fixed yet. When you join this table with the others, you're accidentally duplicating records."

"Ah, so we just need to filter out the duplicates?" I asked, attempting to sound insightful.

"Exactly." Peter tapped the keyboard, adding row numbers over customer IDs to ensure only the first instance of each ID was used. He re-ran the code. Moments later, the inflated counts vanished. The totals aligned perfectly with the official sales report.

I rushed back to Mary's desk.

"Hey, I've got great news," I announced triumphantly. "We figured out the mystery behind the inflated numbers."

Mary looked up, her face a mixture of exhaustion and hope. "Seriously?"

"Yup," I said, turning my laptop screen to face her. "Look at the new numbers."

Her eyes widened as she scanned the results. "They're spot on!"

I copied the updated query from my SQL editor and sent it to her. Moments later, she ran the query on her laptop. This time, it worked flawlessly.

"Thank you so much," she said, relief washing over her face.

"Teamwork makes the dream work," I replied with a grin, walking back to my desk.

Mary's smile was brighter than it had been all day.

***

The Role of Comparative Advantage

The story of Mary's marketing mystery paints a familiar picture of a typical workday, and one that many office workers can relate to. The conversation between Mary and Jim in the kitchen reflects a common workplace scenario: two colleagues so preoccupied with their own tasks that they can't spare time to help one another.

On the surface, Jim's decision to decline Mary's request seems logical. Helping her debug her code would delay the completion of his own project, pushing back the deployment of a new product. From Jim's perspective, prioritizing his own task may seem like the right move – after all, he's responsible for his deadlines. But this reasoning has a critical flaw.

When we step back and look at the broader picture, it becomes clear that Jim's assistance could have benefited the company as a whole. Here's why: Mary's struggle suggests a gap in her technical knowledge or coding experience. In contrast, Jim, being a seasoned analyst, might only need a few minutes to recognize and resolve the issue. The problem with Mary's report wasn't an error in logic or math – it was about duplicate entries in a data source. Mary had no way of knowing this because she wasn't aware of the database's quirks, whereas Jim, through experience or exposure to similar issues, might recognize it instantly.

By taking just 15 minutes to review Mary's code, Jim could have quickly identified the problem, saving Mary hours (or even days) of unproductive effort. While Jim's own project might experience a brief delay, the combined output of both projects would be higher.

This scenario is a classic example of comparative advantage, a concept popularized by British political economist David Ricardo over two centuries ago. Ricardo's theory argues that efficiency is maximized when people (or countries) focus on tasks where they have a relative advantage. Applying this to our example, Jim has a comparative advantage over Mary in debugging code, even if he's also good at other tasks. By focusing on what each person does best – Mary on marketing strategy, Jim on coding, and me on "defending the kitchen" – the team becomes more efficient as a whole.

Of course, in the real world, this logic isn't always so clear-cut. There are unknowns. It's possible Jim could spend hours looking at the code and still not find the problem. It's also possible that Mary could eventually solve the problem herself, albeit more slowly. Another factor to consider is the relative importance of each project. If Jim's deployment task has a massive impact on the company's revenue, it might indeed be the better use of his time. Without a crystal ball, it's hard to predict the "perfect" course of action in every situation. Real-life decisions are messy and depend on many unpredictable variables.

> *Everybody is a genius. But if you judge a fish by its ability to climb a tree, it will live its whole life believing that it is stupid.*
>
> **Albert Einstein**

But let's leave the company's perspective aside for a moment and shift our attention to the employees themselves. How should you, as an employee, handle these situations? How do you decide whether to help a colleague like Mary or focus on your own tasks?

Why Helping Others Helps You Too

One of the strongest indicators of success at work is how others perceive you. Are you seen as intelligent, helpful, trustworthy, and skilled in your field? If the answer is "yes," then you're on a path to success. Interestingly, this perception is often more important than your actual abilities. As seen in the story of Albert Einstein and his driver, being perceived as knowledgeable sometimes matters more than being knowledgeable. The world is full of people with great skills but poor reputations, and they rarely receive the recognition they deserve.

This raises an interesting question: Would Mary's perception of Jim have changed if he had taken 15 minutes to help her?

Admittedly, a single incident may not be enough to alter Mary's view of Jim. But what if it happens repeatedly? What if, on ten separate occasions, Jim provides timely assistance, while another colleague consistently declines to help? It doesn't take a genius to see how those two people would be perceived differently.

I remember two developers, former colleagues of mine, who always made themselves available to help others without hesitation. I never heard them say, "Sorry, I'm too busy" – not even once. This behavior was not common. Most employees fell somewhere in the middle – sometimes helpful, sometimes focused on their own tasks. Then there were those who never made time for others, always citing "busy schedules" as their excuse. You can probably guess who the two most highly respected developers in the company were.

The benefits of being helpful go beyond mere reputation. When you assist others, you project two key traits that people value in the workplace:

1. You are seen as a supportive and caring person.
2. You are perceived as highly skilled in your field.

The first point is simple enough – people appreciate kindness. But the second point requires a little more explanation. Why does helping someone make you look more competent? After all, there may be other colleagues who are even more skilled than you. Here's the catch: The person you help sees your skills in action, but they don't see the skills of colleagues who declined to help or weren't even asked.

Imagine Mary approaches you for help instead of Jim. You review her code, identify the issue, and resolve it. In Mary's mind, this confirms her belief that you are highly skilled. If Jim is actually more skilled than you, it doesn't matter – Mary won't know, because Jim didn't step up to help. This "visibility effect" explains why helpful employees are often perceived as more competent, even when they aren't the most skilled people in the room.

Why Being a Team Player Matters

Being perceived as a "team player" is one of the fastest ways to build a positive workplace reputation. People are more inclined to admire those who support others than those who only look out for themselves. But it is of course not only perceived reputation that team players gain, being a team player is also essential for the success of the entire collective.

To illustrate, let's imagine a scene from a hypothetical basketball game. It's 2022, and the Los Angeles Lakers are playing in front of a packed crowd at the Staples Center. The opposing team misses a shot, and LeBron James pulls down the rebound with ease. Instinctively, he pushes the ball up the court, dribbling with the precision of a surgeon. Three defenders rush to stop him — because he's the only Laker actually participating in the attack — and he takes a tough, contested shot. It bounces off the rim.

Meanwhile, his four Lakers teammates might as well be cardboard cutouts. No screens. No cuts. No off-ball movement. Just four guys in Lakers jerseys standing around like they're waiting for a bus.

Moments later, the opposing team loses possession, and Anthony Davis charges down the court. But it's déjà vu. No movement. No support. No teammates to be found. Two defenders swarm him, cutting off the passing lanes. Just when it seems he's about to lose the ball, he somehow threads a wild pass to Russell Westbrook. Miraculously, it gets through.

Feeling like his shift is over, Davis backs away, clocking out in spirit if not in fact. Westbrook now has the ball. New possession, same old story — no help from his teammates whatsoever — just Westbrook against the entire defense.

Out of options, Westbrook barrels headfirst into the defense like a wrecking ball, flailing past limbs and bodies. Surrounded by defenders, he takes a near-impossible shot and somehow, against all odds, it goes in.

Anyone familiar with the Lakers knows this scenario isn't even remotely accurate. It's not just that LeBron missed while Westbrook made it — the real flaw is the idea that the Lakers are playing 1-on-5 basketball on every possession. In reality, the Lakers thrive on teamwork, movement, and coordination. But in this fantasy world, they're not teammates — they're just wearing the same jersey.

Here, each player takes their turn playing "hero ball" while the rest watch like fans in the front row. They may share the same uniform, but they're not sharing the same mission. If the Lakers played like this in real life, they wouldn't just miss the playoffs — they'd be lucky to win a single game. Because in basketball, five disconnected stars don't make a constellation. They just burn out.

Team sports are remarkably efficient business units, with the workflow of elite teams honed to near perfection. Every player's strengths are maximized, while their weaknesses are skillfully covered by teammates. For nearly two decades, Lionel Messi stood out as a generational talent in football (soccer), especially during his legendary tenure at FC Barcelona. The team strategically channeled their attack through Messi, knowing that his extraordinary dribbling skills and world-class finishing made him a lethal force near the opponent's penalty area. The result? Countless goals, assists, and trophies.

However, even a player as transcendent as Messi wasn't tasked with doing it all. At FC Barcelona, other players rushed to the penalty area during corner kicks because they had a comparative advantage in aerial duels and heading the ball. Likewise, Messi's defensive contributions were kept to a minimum. He was rarely asked to track back or take on defensive duties. Instead, the team's strategy allowed him to conserve energy for offensive play, where his unique talents had the most impact. Other players, better suited for defending, stepped up to fill this gap.

This approach reflects a broader principle seen in elite sports teams: leverage strengths and address weaknesses. Every player contributes according to their comparative advantage. It's a strategy that doesn't just apply to sports — it's a concept that businesses should embrace as well. Just as Lakers and FC Barcelona players strive for victory, employees within a company should rally around a common goal: driving growth and boosting profits. To achieve this, it's essential for each employee to understand their unique role and for workflows to be optimized to extract maximum value from every team member.

However, many companies lag significantly behind top sports teams in fostering a collective mindset. While elite athletes are always attuned to their teammates' roles and ready to offer assistance, typical workplaces often see employees fixated on their own tasks, losing sight of the shared goal. So, how can this disconnect be addressed?

It starts with another ingredient of the success puzzle: When asked a question, assume you are the best person to answer. If someone comes to you for help, it's not by chance or boredom — it's because they believe you're the best person to assist them. If they thought someone else was better suited, they would have gone to that person instead. You better assume they are right until proven otherwise. Providing assistance — or at least pointing them in the direction of someone who can — strengthens trust, improves collaboration, and promotes a smoother workflow across the team.

The Rule of Teamwork:

When asked a question, assume you are the best person to answer.

Why does it work? This principle aligns with the theory of comparative advantage, optimizing the efficiency of a working collective. By embodying this rule, you demonstrate a willingness to help and contribute, enhancing your reputation as a proactive and intelligent team player. People remember those who step up, and they notice those who don't.

Consider the following scenario: Someone approaches you with a problem they've been struggling to solve, believing you have the insight to help. Before they explain the problem, you have no idea how much help you can provide. Instead of sending them away, recognize that the other person has already made that calculation for you. Their decision to ask you wasn't random. In such situations, it's wise to trust their judgment and consider the possibility that you are, in fact, the right person for the job.

Answer the request first; you'll have plenty of time to second-guess yourself later.

It only takes a few moments to assess the problem. In some cases, you may find you have just the right insight to offer a solution, saving both time and frustration. Other times, you may realize you're not equipped to solve the issue — but even then, you can still direct them to a more suitable resource. And here's the kicker: even if you can't fully resolve the problem, your effort will be appreciated. People don't forget those who tried to help, even when the solution wasn't found.

While it may be tempting to prioritize your own tasks and ignore requests for help, it's crucial to resist that urge. Investing a few minutes to understand the problem can yield long-term benefits. First, it contributes to a more collaborative work environment, where knowledge-sharing and problem-solving become the norm. Second, it strengthens your reputation as a supportive and dependable team player.

Unlike the individual effort you pour into your own assignments, helping others is a performance that has an audience. The person you assist directly witnesses your capabilities, while your solitary efforts often go unnoticed. This visibility is an opportunity to make an impression, and that impression can have a lasting impact.

The positive perception you create by being helpful and approachable far outweighs the minimal time investment required. And while you may not be able to help every time, you'll always win points just for trying.

The Problem with "Do Not Disturb" Stickers

At one of the companies I worked for, management introduced a new initiative to reduce interruptions. Each employee received a sticker that read:

"If I'm wearing headphones, I'm busy. Please don't disturb me. Ping me in Slack instead. "

The idea was simple: if you needed uninterrupted focus, slap on the sticker, pop on your headphones, and voilà — instant privacy. No awkward "can I bother you for a second?" moments.

The stickers were a hit. Soon, half the office was wearing headphones, not just to focus but to subtly signal, "Don't even think about talking to me."

While the stickers brought some positives in the form of less interruptions, they created another problem. With everyone "headphoned in," collaboration took a hit. People stopped reaching out for help. The energy of teamwork slowly drained from the office. Slack messages became the new interruptions, but unlike face-to-face chats, they could be ignored indefinitely.

It's easy to see why this happened. In a world of constant notifications and information overload, focus is hard to come by. So, naturally, everyone wants to protect it. But here's the irony — in their quest for focus, employees unknowingly isolate themselves from opportunities to collaborate, build relationships, and offer help.

Yes, you might finish your project a bit faster. But what did you miss in those extra 15 minutes? A chance to be seen as a team player. A moment to help a teammate in need. An opportunity to reinforce your reputation as "the person who always helps."

Finishing work a little faster won't get you a standing ovation. But being known as "the person who always helps" — that will follow you for years.

Given my attitude toward these stickers, do you think I refused mine? Of course not. I accepted it, but I made a small modification. I took out a pen, crossed out the original message, and replaced it with: "If I'm wearing headphones, it means the fire alarm is doing its daily rehearsal."

It was a joke – but also a reflection of my approach. I never wear headphones at work because I want to stay available for those who need help. The only time I make an exception is when the fire alarm goes off for no good reason.

The Final Takeaway

When asked a question, assume you are the best person to answer. The king's advisor from the beginning of the chapter failed to follow this principle, and as a result, his unmatched expertise went to waste. Despite being the foremost authority on trade, his reluctance to engage cost him his influence. Jim risks a similar fate if he continues to brush off his colleagues' requests.

In contrast, I've lived by this rule for years – and I can confidently say it's paid off. By consistently being seen as helpful and competent (occasionally more than deserved), I've earned the trust and appreciation of my colleagues. Being viewed as someone who is capable, supportive, and reliable is a significant measure of success.

In the corporate world, crucial decisions – like raises, promotions, and layoffs – are often made with incomplete information. When managers lack a complete picture, the perceptions they hold about employees become a deciding factor. This is why it's essential to cultivate a positive and lasting impression. Maybe that's why, despite my 'extended kitchen hours,' I've never been laid off.

***

At 5 p.m., Mary gathers her belongings and heads for the exit. As she passes my desk, she pauses. "Good evening, Andres," she says warmly, her voice a blend of exhaustion and gratitude. "I really appreciate your help. I couldn't have managed without you." Her sincere thanks are a clear sign of the impact I made. It's obvious that she now sees me as a dependable source of support — and maybe, just maybe, she'll come to me before Jim the next time she needs help.

"Good evening," I reply with a smile. "It was a pleasure to help. See you tomorrow."

Mary glances back at me with a sly grin. "See you tomorrow ... in the kitchen."

***

The Rule of Teamwork:

When asked a question, assume you are the best person to answer.

Chapter 9

The Meta Level Trick

When we strive to become better than we are, everything around us becomes better too.

Paulo Coelho, The Alchemist

The Horseshoe Paradox

Danish physicist, Nobel Prize winner, and pioneer of quantum theory Niels Bohr was renowned for his groundbreaking contributions to atomic structure. Despite his deep-rooted commitment to rationality and empirical science, an intriguing story circulated about him that raised a few eyebrows. Above the entrance to his home hung a horseshoe — a symbol of good luck in many European countries, including Denmark, where it's believed to ward off evil spirits.

One day, a friend visiting Bohr noticed the horseshoe and, puzzled by the contradiction, asked, "Do you really believe the horseshoe brings good luck?"

Bohr, ever the scientist, replied, "Of course not! I'm a scientist; I don't put stock in such superstitions."

His friend, even more perplexed, pressed further, "Then why do you have it there?"

Bohr leaned in with a sly grin and said, "I was told it works even if you don't believe in it!

***

Lessons from the Board Game Table

In the strategic board game *Catan,* negotiation is a pivotal skill that can make or break a player's success. When a 7 is rolled or a Knight card is played, the "robber" enters the scene, allowing the active player to steal a card from another player. This sparks a flurry of negotiations as players try to influence the thief's target. Strong diplomatic skills give a player a distinct edge, often tipping the scales of the entire game in their favor.

During a *Catan* session with friends, I had a front-row seat to an extraordinary demonstration of this principle. Martin, a skilled player and former National Champion, took an early lead. Typically, in *Catan,* the player in the lead becomes the prime target for theft and sabotage. However, to everyone's surprise, a new player at the table consistently avoided targeting Martin, even when given the perfect opportunity.

As Martin's lead widened, it became clear that the most effective strategy for the rest of us was to work together and steal from him at every chance. Yet, the new player remained stubbornly independent, refusing to participate in the plan.

After Martin's decisive victory, we took a break. I approached the new player to ask about her strategy. Her response caught me completely off guard:

"Oh, you know, he's just so likable. I didn't want to steal from him!"

That's when it hit me — being likable is an advantage in *Catan,* especially in casual games with players who don't follow strict game theory. But there's a crucial nuance: the longer you maintain kindness, generosity, and likability, the longer it benefits you. A brief flash of charm isn't enough. If you want to benefit from being seen as "the nice player" for the entire game, you have to stay likable for the entire game. This revelation left me wondering: could the same logic apply to other board games — or even to real life?

It shouldn't come as a surprise that, at certain moments — weddings, job interviews, your child's birthday, or other special occasions — we all strive to be better than usual. If you think you're an exception, just think back to how you behaved on your first date. Were you more polite, more attentive, more thoughtful than usual? I'm willing to bet you were.

Of course, in those moments, we're not actually "better people" — we're just *appearing* to be better. It's a performance — a temporary play-act meant to impress. Our "real self" is waiting in the wings, ready to step back into the spotlight as soon as the performance ends. But here's the key insight: if you behave like a better version of yourself, even for a short time, then in that moment, you *are* a better version of yourself.

Think about it. If you isolate those few hours from the rest of your life — as if the rest of your life didn't exist — then, during that window, there is no "appearing better" because there's nothing to compare it to. For that period, you are genuinely a better person. This subtle shift in perspective unlocks a powerful philosophical thought experiment.

What happens if we extend that play-act? Suppose we don't just "perform" for a single day but for an entire month. If you manage to stay consistent for a month, you may already start seeing tangible results — people might like you more, trust you more, or even view you as a better person. But of course, in your mind, it would still feel like a "performance," with your "true self" lurking in the background, waiting for its chance to return.

But why stop there?

Remember the lesson from *Catan*: to maximize your chances, you can't just be likable for part of the game — you have to be likable for the entire game. So, what if we applied this logic to life as a whole? What if, instead of "performing" for a few days, weeks, or even months, you stayed in your "play-act" indefinitely — not for a part of your life but for *all* of it?

Here's where it gets interesting. If the "act" never ends — if there's no "rest of your life" to contrast it with — then the play-act becomes your entire life. And at that point, the line between "acting better" and "being better" disappears.

If you never stop the act, it stops being an act. You're not pretending to be a better person anymore; you *are* a better person.

Why We're Blind to Our Own Problems

Above all, don't lie to yourself. **Fyodor Dostoevsky**

We all agree that becoming a better person is a worthy pursuit. But here's the real challenge: How do we do it? What exactly needs to change, and why? The answer might seem obvious, but it's not. The truth is, humans are remarkably bad at recognizing the need for change in their own lives. And if we can't identify what needs improvement, how can we expect to improve at all?

To illustrate this point, I conducted a small experiment with twenty friends. I asked them a simple but revealing question:

"What is the single worst aspect of your life that you have the power to change?"

The answers were both predictable and telling. The most common complaint, cited by seven out of twenty people, was a "terrible boss." Next in line were "dull jobs" and "unhappy relationships," each with five votes. A few mentioned financial struggles, while one friend sarcastically listed an "annoying friend who gives me stupid tests." I sincerely hope she was joking.

But here's where things get interesting. I asked a follow-up question:

"Do you plan to do anything to address this issue in the next three months?"

The results were shocking. Seventeen out of twenty participants said no. Only three indicated they had any intention of taking action — and one of them was the person jokingly complaining about the "irritating friend." Not a single person with an unhappy relationship planned to do anything about it.

For the final part of the experiment, I presented them with a twist:

"Imagine your best friend is facing the exact same problem that you identified as the worst aspect of your own life. Should they try to change it within the next three months?"

This time, the responses were unanimous. Every single person said yes. Every. Single. One.

The exercise highlighted something profound: We are far more willing to recognize the need for change in other people's lives than in our own. We have no problem spotting flaws in other people's decisions, yet we resist seeing them in ourselves. Why? Because we are all lying to ourselves. If you think you don't, you're lying to yourself.

We convince ourselves that things are "fine" even when, deep down, we know they aren't. It's a coping mechanism that protects us from discomfort but also traps us in mediocrity.

Enter the Meta Level

It's time to introduce a concept that can help you overcome the blind spots in your thinking and stop lying to yourself: a clever strategy I call the "meta level trick." Imagine the meta level as a bird's-eye view of your life, a vantage point from which you can observe yourself with complete objectivity, the way an impartial judge would. But this judge isn't here to criticize you. This judge genuinely wants you to succeed. From this higher perspective, it becomes much easier to spot which qualities you need to develop and which weaknesses you need to overcome. Think of it as having your own personal life coach who is immune to excuses, blind spots, and self-deception.

If you've ever seen *The Matrix*, you might recognize a similar concept. There's a famous scene where Trinity needs to pilot a helicopter, but she doesn't know how. So Tank, from the control room, uploads a helicopter piloting program directly into her brain. Seconds later, she opens her eyes and says, "I know how to fly a helicopter." The meta level works like the control room. No, it can't upload a helicopter piloting program directly into your brain, but it does offer something just as powerful: the ability to recognize what's wrong in your life, what you need to master and why it matters. From the meta level, you see yourself with clarity – free from ego, excuses, and self-delusion – making it far easier to identify what actually needs to change.

The meta level is just the ability to see your life as if you were a third-party observer. The goal of this approach is simple: identify areas where you need to improve yourself (like becoming kinder or less greedy) and recognize where changes are needed in your life (like dealing with a toxic boss or leaving an unhappy relationship). A useful way to approach self-improvement is to think of yourself as a collection of roles you play in life: partner, parent, employee, friend, customer, neighbor, citizen, and so on. Each role requires different qualities, so it's helpful to reflect on which role needs the most improvement right now. Once you've identified the role that needs the most attention, you can pinpoint the specific quality to work on. Here are a few examples:

- As a parent, you might want to improve patience and kindness.
- As a friend, you might focus on being more supportive and reliable.
- As a partner, you may strive to show more compassion, empathy, and love.
- As an employee, you might aim to boost your efficiency, improve technical skills, or become more proactive.

The key insight here is that the qualities you need to improve depend on the role you're focused on. Your toddler doesn't care about your technical skills, just as your boss has little reason to retain unproductive employees solely because they are kind and patient. By identifying the role that requires attention, you can direct your efforts where they'll have the greatest impact.

The Rule of the Meta Level:

Look at your life from a distance as if it were somebody else's life. That's how you recognize what needs to change. Program yourself to become a better person and convince your everyday self to address the things you're most unhappy with.

Why does it work? Because we are biased and far from objective about our own lives. The meta level allows us to step outside ourselves, making it possible to identify and address not only our personal shortcomings but also the broader issues in our lives.

Tapping into the meta level is an incredibly powerful concept. It can challenge your beliefs on the primary level, sometimes in surprising ways. Even Niels Bohr, the renowned physicist known for his scientific rigor, entertained the idea that a horseshoe might bring luck.

This story reveals a curious truth about human nature: we often act in ways that defy our logical beliefs. You might not believe in God but still live as if one exists (as I do). You might insist that talent is a myth, even though most experts disagree. And you may not believe in the luck-bringing power of a horseshoe, but that doesn't stop you from hanging one up "just in case."

These actions may seem contradictory, but they're not. The meta level allows us to prioritize effectiveness over rigid logic. The primary-level self may focus on being rational, but the meta self focuses on being effective. And that, in the end, is what drives real change.

If you are not sure how to go to the meta level, here is a simple exercise to start with. Take five minutes to list out the most important roles in your life. For each role, write down one quality you want to improve. Then ask yourself, "What would a better version of me do in that role tomorrow?"

The rule of the meta level tells you *what* needs to be improved, but it doesn't always tell you *how*. However, once the meta level has identified the improvement, it becomes your new goal — and if you've been following this book, you already know the *how* part.

The Horseshoe's Final Lesson

To wrap up this chapter, I have to say that the meta level is one of the most profound concepts in this entire book. My hope is that I've persuaded you to believe in it. But even if I haven't, that's okay too. You should still use the rule of the meta level. Why?

Because, just like Niels Bohr's horseshoe, it works even if you don't believe in it.

***

The Rule of the Meta Level:

Look at your life from a distance as if it were somebody else's life. That's how you recognize what needs to change. Program yourself to become a better person and convince your everyday self to address the things you're most unhappy with.

Chapter 10

In the Footsteps of Agent Mulder

Smart people learn from everything and everyone, average people from their experiences, stupid people already have all the answers.

Socrates

The Mushroom of Doubt

"Scully, we never escaped. We're still trapped underground."

— Agent Fox Mulder

In an underground cave. Trapped by a giant, mind-bending mushroom. Controlled by hallucinations so vivid, you'd swear they were real. This was no ordinary day for Agents Mulder and Scully of *The X-Files*.

After what felt like an eternity, Mulder fought his way out of the cave, dragging Scully behind him. Back at FBI headquarters, they met with their boss, Assistant Director Walter Skinner, to report on their encounter with the mushroom – a strange organism that used hallucinogenic spores to lure prey into its lair.

But something wasn't right.

As Mulder sat in Skinner's office, a disturbing realization struck him. He glanced at his hands, then at Scully. Neither of them had any injuries – not even a scratch – despite having spent hours submerged in digestive acid. It didn't add up. The story, the escape, the entire sequence of events – something was off.

That's when it hit him.

"Scully, we never escaped," Mulder said, his voice sharp with conviction. "We're still trapped underground."

Scully frowned, clearly unconvinced. "Mulder, we did escape," she replied firmly. "I think you're suffering from post-traumatic stress."

But Mulder's eyes narrowed with certainty. "No, I'm not," he said, his voice steady and resolute. "This is not real. YOU are not real."

Scully shook her head, unwilling to accept his theory. She dismissed his concerns — until Mulder took matters into his own hands.

"I'll prove it to you," he said, pulling out his gun. Before anyone could react, he fired a shot directly into Skinner's chest.

For a moment, there was silence.

Then, instead of blood, a thick, yellow goo oozed from the bullet wounds.

Scully's eyes widened in horror as the illusion shattered around them. Their surroundings dissolved, and they found themselves back in the dark, humid depths of the cave. Once again, they were lying on the cold, damp ground, surrounded by the colossal, pulsating mushrooms. The truth was undeniable — their "escape" had been nothing but a hallucination.

Mulder's doubt was their only weapon against the illusion. His refusal to trust what he saw had allowed them to see through it. But the victory was short-lived. As they tried to get their bearings, another hallucination quickly enveloped them. The cycle had restarted. Once again, the agents were trapped in a new false reality, unable to break free except in their minds.

Eventually, an FBI rescue team pulled them from the cave, but it was Mulder's relentless questioning that gave them a fighting chance.

(The X-Files, Season 6, Episode 21)

***

The 3-Step Agent Mulder Method

"Trust no one. Deny everything. The truth is out there."

This iconic phrase from *The X-Files* perfectly captures the show's essence. In a world where conspiracies lurk in every shadow, Agents Mulder and Scully are in constant pursuit of the elusive truth. But their mission is anything but straightforward.

Each encounter is a test of perception and logic, where nothing can be taken at face value. Their mantra is simple: question everything. Nobody can be trusted to tell you the truth. The truth is buried, distorted, and denied — but it is out there, waiting to be found.

But how do you actually find it?

Enter the 3-Step Agent Mulder Method. It's a mental framework for spotting, challenging, and testing assumptions to uncover the truth. Inspired by the actions of Mulder himself, this method can help you escape false realities in your own life — whether they involve bad decisions, flawed logic, or the illusions created by others.

The 3 Steps to Uncover the Truth

- Step 1: Spot the assumption (The Mulder Moment)
- Step 2: Challenge the assumption (The Scully Challenge)
- Step 3: Replace the assumption with a test (The Skinner Shot)

The Mulder Moment is the spark of doubt — that sudden, subtle realization that something doesn't add up. In the Mushroom of Doubt story, it happens when Mulder notices that neither he nor

Scully have any injuries, despite being drenched in digestive acid. If their story of escaping the cave were true, they should have injuries or at least signs of a struggle. But there's nothing.

The Scully Challenge is when you actively challenge the assumption. You don't just "notice something is off" — you act on it. You analyze, question, or confront the story directly. In the Mushroom of Doubt, the Scully Challenge happens when Mulder calls out Scully's belief that they escaped. He actively questions her, even when she resists.

The Skinner Shot is when you verify reality. It's the ultimate check — an action that delivers hard, indisputable evidence. In the Mushroom of Doubt, the Skinner Shot is literal: Mulder fires a shot at Skinner. This is the moment of absolute proof. If Skinner bleeds, the story is real. If something else happens, then it's an illusion.

These three steps form a complete framework for identifying illusions and exposing reality. Let's see how they apply to three new stories.

Spot the Assumption (The Mulder Moment)

Trench Board Game Story

Years ago, I was involved in developing an online version of the board game Trench. The development team had created an early version of the app, which I tested four months before the first tournament was scheduled.

At first glance, I was blown away. The graphics were stunning. Players could rotate the board in every direction — up, down, left, right, and every angle in between. It was a visual spectacle.

But something felt off.

While exploring the app, I noticed there was no standard top-down view — a basic feature found on every online board game platform. The 360-degree rotation was flashy, but it had a downside: parts of the board would slide out of view, making it difficult to see all the pieces at once.

That was my moment of doubt, the Mulder Moment. I spotted the inconsistency. The absence of a top-down view didn't add up. This was a sign that something was wrong.

But I ignored it. I dismissed it as a temporary oversight that would be fixed. After all, I figured, every experienced board game player knows that a clear top-down view is essential. Surely, the developers knew this too. This was my flawed assumption. I trusted that "they knew what they were doing" and moved on.

Three months later, I tested the app again. The 360-degree view was still there, but the top-down view was still missing. The same issue I had noticed three months earlier remained unresolved. Frustrated, I reached out to the developers and asked what they had been working on.

They proudly presented a list of flashy new features: extra customization options, advanced graphics, and quirky sound effects. None of it addressed the missing top-down view. The ability to rotate the board at all angles felt more like a magician's trick than a practical feature. Pieces would slide out of view like Houdini disappearing from the stage. As for the sound effects, they were extravagant but pointless. All I really needed was a simple top-down view and a few basic sound alerts, but it wasn't there.

This was the moment I finally challenged my assumption, the Scully Challenge. I no longer trusted the idea that "they know what they're doing." I confronted the developers and asked them directly, "Why is there still no top-down view?"

But I didn't stop there. I followed up with one simple question that changed everything: "Have any of you ever played a board game before?"

They hadn't. None of them. That was the Skinner Shot. The truth was revealed. The developers admitted they had never played a board game in their lives. This was my hard evidence. My assumption – that they knew what they were doing – had been shattered. The moment they confessed this, my previous doubts were fully validated. My Mulder Moment was correct. My Scully Challenge was justified. The Skinner Shot had landed.

Looking back, I know exactly where I went wrong. I ignored the Mulder Moment. I noticed the missing top-down view, but I dismissed it. I assumed the developers knew what they were doing, even when the evidence suggested otherwise. If I had acted on that doubt three months earlier, I could have confronted the team much sooner. I could have executed the Scully Challenge in week one instead of month four. I could have asked a single, simple question: "Have any of you ever played a board game before?"

If I had done that, I would have received my Skinner Shot answer much earlier, and everything that followed would have changed.

"Assumption is the mother of all f*ckups," as Casey Ryback, played by Steven Seagal, famously said in *Under Siege 2*. The phrase holds a vital truth: Never assume that something is true just because it seems so at first glance. Ask yourself: *Is it really true?* If I had asked that question earlier, I would have seen that my assumption – that the developers understood board games – was false. The truth was out there, but I missed it because I failed to act on my own doubt.

Challenge the Assumption (The Scully Challenge)

The "Obvious" Move

Back in my university years, there was a café in my hometown of Tartu called Werner. Known for its rich chess history, it boasted a table with a chessboard that constantly drew players seeking a challenge. For the regulars, it was a battleground of wits where anyone could prove their strategic prowess.

On one memorable afternoon, a master player sat at the board, drawing a crowd with his skillful play. One by one, he dispatched his opponents with apparent ease. But during one particular game, something unusual happened — the master paused to think.

"What's there to think about for so long?" someone from the audience blurted out. "Rook to H4 — it's obvious!"

All eyes turned toward the speaker. It was a local player of mediocre strength, certainly no candidate master. The self-assurance in his voice was unshakable. I glanced at the board and, to my surprise, saw that Rook to H4 did indeed look like a strong move. But was it the strongest?

This was the master's Mulder Moment. The crowd may have been swayed by the confident suggestion, but the master wasn't. He spotted the trap — just because something looks obvious doesn't mean it's right. While the crowd assumed it was the best move, the master spotted it was just an assumption and not necessarily the truth.

The master challenged the assumption. Instead of playing Rook to H4 immediately (as the crowd expected), he went into a deep reflection. His elbows rested on the table, his hands cradled his head, and his eyes scanned the board with laser focus. This was the Scully Challenge in action. While the crowd saw simplicity, the master saw complexity. He wasn't looking for a move that was tempting — he was searching for the best move.

Moments passed. The audience grew impatient. The local player fidgeted, clearly thinking, "Why is he taking so long? I already told him the best move!" But the master ignored the noise. He continued his analysis, searching for alternatives.

Then it happened. The Skinner Shot. The master made his decision. Slowly, he reached for a piece — but it wasn't the rook. Instead, he slid his knight to G5. It wasn't flashy, but it was brilliant. The crowd murmured in surprise. This move displayed a depth of strategic thinking that none of us had seen — certainly not the local player.

At this point, the test had been fired. The Skinner Shot was in motion. The board itself would provide the result. If the master's Knight to G5 move succeeded in giving him a strategic edge, his challenge of the crowd's suggestion would be validated.

In this story, the Scully Challenge is the most pivotal moment. It's where the master pauses, reflects, and resists the pressure of the crowd's confidence. Without this moment of doubt, he would have blindly played Rook to H4.

The difference between the master and the local player wasn't chess skill alone. It was how they approached doubt. The master did what the local player couldn't:

- He noticed the Mulder Moment.
- He executed the Scully Challenge by questioning the "obvious."
- He fired the Skinner Shot and put his theory to the ultimate test.

This is why the master won another game, and the local player was left pretending he had never spoken at all.

Test the Assumption (The Skinner Shot)

The Lawyer's Great Escape (Almost)

It sounds like the start of a classic joke: A doctor, a lawyer, a priest, and a little boy are on a plane. Suddenly, disaster strikes. The engines fail, and the plane begins to plummet.

The pilot grabs a parachute, shouts, "Every man for himself!" and jumps out of the plane.

Scrambling for survival, the boy finds a bag of parachutes and places them on his lap. But there's a problem — there are only three parachutes left for the four remaining passengers.

The doctor wastes no time. He snatches one of the parachutes and declares, "I'm a doctor! People need me to save lives!" And with that, he leaps from the plane.

Next up is the lawyer. With an air of self-importance, he snatches a bag from the boy's lap and boasts, "I'm a lawyer, and lawyers are the smartest people in the world. I have to survive!" Without a second thought, he leaps from the plane.

That leaves only the priest and the boy. The priest lets out a heavy sigh and looks at the boy. "Son," he says softly, "I'm old. I've lived a full life. You're young and have your whole life ahead of you. Take the last parachute. You deserve to live."

But the boy grins and says, "Don't worry, Father. We'll both survive. The 'smartest person in the world' just jumped out with my backpack."

What went wrong for the lawyer?

The lawyer had no Mulder Moment. When he grabbed the bag, he didn't notice anything was off. There was no sense of doubt, no sense that something wasn't right. A potential Mulder Moment could have occurred if he had sensed something strange — the texture of the bag, the weight, or the absence of shoulder straps. But he missed all these potential clues. His confidence blinded him to doubt.

Because he skipped the Mulder Moment, he never had a chance to engage in the next step — the Scully Challenge. He didn't question his belief that "this bag is a parachute". In fact, he didn't challenge any of his assumptions:

- He assumed the bag was a parachute.
- He assumed he didn't need to check it.
- He assumed he was too smart to be wrong.

Had he done even the smallest Scully Challenge, he could have caught his mistake. All he had to do was:

- Check the weight of the bag (backpacks are lighter than parachutes).
- Check for straps (backpacks have thin straps, parachutes have thick shoulder harnesses).
- Look for the pull cord (parachutes have a prominent pull handle).

Each of these actions would have been a Skinner Shot. Each would have validated his belief being wrong. But he skipped it. He let arrogance drive his decision.

But if you are not firing the Skinner Shot yourself, this doesn't mean it doesn't happen. It just doesn't happen on your terms. With no Mulder Moment and no Scully Challenge, the lawyer walked straight into the Skinner Shot. But this time, it was reality firing the shot, not him.

The Skinner Shot that followed was simple: either he pulled a cord and floated safely to the ground, or he didn't. The result of the test? Gravity delivered it.

What should the lawyer have done?

Had he stopped for even two seconds, the story would have changed. If he had just felt the weight of the bag, looked for the pull cord, or checked for the straps, he would have caught his mistake. But he skipped every possible checkpoint.

This story perfectly illustrates that the Skinner Shot will happen whether you like it or not. Gravity doesn't care about your assumptions. Reality will always give you a Skinner Shot, whether you're ready for it or not.

The lawyer's downfall wasn't just bad luck — it was overconfidence. If you think you're the smartest person in the room, you stop listening, stop questioning, and stop learning. His entitlement and self-importance led to his downfall. Literally.

The lesson? You can skip the Mulder Moment. You can skip the Scully Challenge. But the Skinner Shot will still come.

Reality always delivers it. And, if you skip the first two steps, you're not in control of the shot. Reality is.

There is a fine line between confidence and overconfidence. For the lawyer, that line was about 20,000 feet in the air.

The Rule of Agent Mulder:

> *The only true wisdom is in knowing that you know nothing.*
>
> **Socrates**

Question everything. Spot the assumption, challenge it, and test it. If the story doesn't add up, it's probably not true.

Why does it work? If you never question what you see and hear, you'll never know more than what you see and hear. This is the heart of the rule of Agent Mulder. It works because illusions collapse under pressure, but only if you apply that pressure.

To see how it works in practice, let me share one final story — one from my own life.

How I Became the Best in Entropy

When I started seriously competing in the game of Entropy, I had a simple strategy: copy the best.

I spent countless hours studying the games of top players. I memorized their opening moves, analyzed their decision-making, and absorbed every strategy they used. This approach worked — at least at first. By emulating the greats, I elevated my game to a level comparable to theirs. It was enough to beat all the weaker players, but there was one problem: I wasn't beating the best. I had become their equal, but never their superior.

The reason is clear now, but at the time, I couldn't see it. The problem was that I was following what others did. There was nothing in my game that other top players didn't have. I was a follower, not a leader.

Then I experienced my Mulder Moment.

The moment of doubt came after yet another match where I lost to a top player, even though I had perfectly followed all the "golden rules" of Entropy. I realized that something was off. I had done everything "correctly," but I still lost. This realization triggered the Mulder Moment: "If I'm following all the 'correct' rules, why am I not winning?"

This was my signal that something about the "golden rules" wasn't as golden as I'd been led to believe.

The Scully Challenge came next.

I decided to challenge the most sacred assumption of Entropy strategy — an idea that had been accepted as gospel for years. I challenged the "golden rule" of balance between the victory points and mobility.

So, I put the assumption under fire. I asked myself: "What happens if I stop following the balance rule? What if I deliberately shift toward mobility over points?"

This was the Scully Challenge in action. I didn't just "think" about it — I put it to the test.

The Skinner Shot was my moment of truth. I didn't just theorize. I executed. I tested my theory in live competition. I shifted my strategy to prioritize mobility over victory points. I played match after match with this new approach. I analyzed every game, noting the results. I tracked every win, every loss, and every advantage. This was my Skinner Shot — the test that would either confirm or refute my new strategy.

The result? It worked.

My unconventional strategy gave me a unique edge over other players who still followed the "golden rules" without question. I wasn't just copying the best anymore — I was becoming the best.

Looking back, I can see the full 3-Step Agent Mulder Method in action:

- The Mulder Moment: Noticing that following the golden rules wasn't getting me wins.
- The Scully Challenge: Challenging the sacred balance between victory points and mobility.
- The Skinner Shot: Testing my theory in live competition to see if it worked.

This method didn't just help me become a champion. It taught me one of the most profound lessons of my life: Copying the best only gets you to their level – never beyond it. If you want to rise above, you have to challenge the rules everyone else follows.

The 3-Step Agent Mulder Method had just claimed another victory.

The Final Truth

> *You know nothing for sure ... except the fact that you know nothing for sure.*
>
> **J. F. Kennedy**

Once you've mastered the first nine rules, success will come naturally. The tenth rule is a bonus that separates the "pretty good" from the "world-class."

Question everything – it's a call to be like Agent Mulder from *The X-Files*. It's a call to trust no one without evidence. It's a call to deny everything that doesn't add up. And most importantly, it's a call to realize that the truth is out there – and to seek it.

When you spot, challenge, and test, you unlock a power that most people never access: the power to see through illusions:

Don't follow the script. Burn it.
Don't accept the story. Break it.
Don't just play the game. Change it.
The truth is out there. Go find it.

***

The Rule of Agent Mulder:

Question everything. Spot the assumption, challenge it, and test it. If the story doesn't add up, it's probably not true.

Summary: Fitting the Pieces of Success Together

Many of life's failures are people who did not realize how close they were to success when they gave up.

Thomas A. Edison

A Toast to Wit: Churchill's Sharpest Comeback

Two great British politicians, Sir Winston Churchill and Lady Astor, were known for their legendary rivalry and sharp exchanges of wit. On one occasion, after being especially annoyed by Churchill, Lady Astor declared,

"Winston, if you were my husband, I would poison your tea!"

To which Churchill, ever the master of the comeback, replied, "Madam, if you were my wife, I would drink it!"

***

The Final Piece: Completing the Puzzle of Success

Assembling a puzzle without all its pieces is an exercise in frustration. Now, having explored the ten chapters of this book, you hold all the essential pieces needed to complete the puzzle of success. Each chapter introduced a fundamental rule — each a vital component of the bigger picture. Below is a recap of these rules, forming the foundation for achieving your goals:

1. **The Rule of Curiosity**: Do what sparks your interest and creates value.
2. **The Rule of Talent**: Assume that talent doesn't exist. It's not a prerequisite for success.
3. **The Rule of the Comfort Zone**: Leave your comfort zone only if you're dissatisfied with your life. Then, work to

expand your comfort zone to make your new challenges feel routine.

4. **The Rule of the Red Ferrari**: Rehearse for event-related goals so you remain in control when it matters most.
5. **The Rule of Long-Term Goals**: Set a long-term goal that describes a desired outcome one to ten years from now or defines a process to achieve it.
6. **The Rule of Stupidity**: Don't believe that success is far away. The belief that others are far smarter than you is a lie; it doesn't take much to catch up with them.
7. **The Rule of Teamwork**: When asked a question, assume you're the best person to answer it.
8. **The Rule of Decision-Making**: Identify the real problem, then use backward induction to determine the action points that will solve it.
9. **The Rule of the Meta-Level**: View your life from a bird's-eye perspective and judge yourself as if you were a neutral observer. Then, program improvements into your "primary self."
10. **The Rule of Agent Mulder**: Question everything and discard what doesn't add up.

With all ten pieces in your hands, the time has come to assemble the puzzle. But having the rules isn't enough — their true power lies in how they work together. To bring this to life, let's explore how the first five rules (with a little help from the sixth and ninth) combine to tackle a relatable goal: learning to play the violin.

How the First Five Rules Work Together: The Violin Example

Imagine you're an analyst at a large corporation, happily married and contemplating expanding your family. You currently live in a cozy rental apartment, but you and your spouse dream of owning a larger home. Despite both having above-average salaries, saving for a down payment has been slow. Your typical workday involves eight hours at the office, followed by evenings spent cooking, watching TV, or occasionally meeting friends for drinks. Your life is stable, but it feels monotonous. Meanwhile, your friends have formed a band and perform at local venues – their lives seem vibrant, full of energy, and just a little more colorful than yours.

One magical evening, your partner surprises you with tickets to a concert featuring none other than violin virtuoso Vanessa Mae. Her breathtaking performance stirs something deep within you – not just admiration for her skill, but also for the soul-stirring sound of the violin. The idea of mastering the violin tugs at your heartstrings (pun intended). Yet, you're reminded of how your accomplished pianist parents always nudged you to follow in their footsteps – a path you set aside but can't quite shake off.

Now, you stand at a crossroads. Should you:

1. Continue down your current path and change nothing,
2. Pursue your newfound passion for the violin, or
3. Strive to fulfill your parents' expectations by playing the piano?

Before deciding, it's wise to gather more information. You reach out to your band friends to see if they need an extra hand. To your delight, they're looking for a violinist, though their repertoire isn't suited for piano, narrowing your options. Pursuing piano now feels misguided, especially considering your lack of curiosity. Investing time in learning piano would likely lead to disappointment – much like my unsuccessful attempts at mastering C# programming. It simply wouldn't work out. You'd commit the error of doing something that shouldn't be done at all.

The Rule of Curiosity

When it comes to the violin, you feel a genuine pull to explore this new adventure — unlike with the piano. That's a curiosity box checked. If you're going to pick up a musical instrument, it should be the violin, not the piano. Two options remain: devote yourself to the violin or stick with your comfortable routine.

The Rule of Comfort Zone (and a touch of the Rule of Meta-Level)

Now we're in comfort zone territory. If your current life were thrilling, you wouldn't have any reason to make it more uncomfortable. But if your existence feels as exciting as watching paint dry, it's time to slip out of your comfort zone and embrace the challenge of learning the violin.

Dreams aren't meant to linger on the shelf. They're meant to be pursued. Looking at your life from a meta-level perspective makes this painfully clear. Imagine it's your best friend asking for your advice. Would you encourage them to keep living the same humdrum life or to chase their dream of learning the violin? You already know the answer. It's time to take that advice yourself. Forget stockpiling house funds for the next ice age. Head to the music store and buy a violin before your partner talks you out of it.

The Rule of Talent

Armed with a shiny new violin and a treasure trove of YouTube tutorials, you dive into the world of violin mastery. You start with the basics: how to grip the bow, where to position the violin, and how to adjust the tuning pegs. After some theory, it's all about practice.

Two months of determined effort later, you still feel like you're paddling in the shallow end compared to your violinist friend Paul. Doubts creep in, and imposter syndrome gnaws at your resolve. You wonder if you simply lack the talent to become as good as Paul. Perhaps studying the violin was a mistake, and you should call it a day.

Hold up!

Talent is a mirage. Feeling "less talented" than Paul is an illusion. Paul wrestled with the same beginner hurdles you're facing. Talent is just a convenient excuse for quitting, and the only reason Paul is better than you is that he has studied and practiced it more. Every master was once a beginner, and Paul is no exception. If you put in as much effort as Paul did, you can reach his level.

Don't hide behind the misconception of talent. It's not a real thing, it's one of the most dangerous lies ever told. Yes, it's easy to retreat into your old life, blaming your "lack of talent" for quitting. But that's not what successful people do. If you quit, it's not because you lack talent, it's because you are a lazy sore loser.

The Rule of Stupidity Meets the Rule of the Red Ferrari

Even if you avoid the talent trap, you might still think that achieving violin mastery requires an impossible amount of effort. This is where the Rule of Stupidity and the Rule of the Red Ferrari come to the rescue.

It's tough to stay motivated if you feel like you're scaling Mount Everest. But here's the truth: it's not a mountain – it's a hill. And you don't even need to reach the summit. Sure, Vanessa Mae inspired you, but you don't have to become Vanessa Mae. Your aim is to blend into a hobby band, not headline Carnegie Hall.

Your friends will gladly welcome you into the band if you're on their level – and they're amateurs like you. The only reason they seem better is that you're just getting started. On a relative scale, you may be behind, but on an absolute scale, the difference is small.

The Rule of Comfort Zone Strikes Again

You've conquered your doubts and committed to mastering the violin. Determined to make progress, you vow to practice "whenever you have time." You read textbooks, watch tutorials, and ask Paul for advice. You're putting in the effort, but something feels off. The process is starting to feel like a grind. Your workflow feels dull and unrewarding. Exhaustion creeps in.

What went wrong?

Here's the issue: you ventured outside your comfort zone to acquire violin skills, but you didn't bring them back into your comfort zone. Instead, you stayed in "challenge mode" for months. This is a recipe for burnout. The goal of leaving the comfort zone is to return with new skills in tow and integrate them into your daily routine.

What should you have done differently?

"Practicing whenever you have time" is not a strategy. "Whenever you have time" often means rarely, or never. It's too random, too unreliable, and too dependent on willpower. Willpower is a finite resource, and once it runs out, progress stops.

Your violin practice needs to be regular and frequent. You could practice once a week — if you have a century to wait. But daily practice is better. When violin practice becomes part of your daily routine, music seeps into your comfort zone. Your learning process becomes smoother and faster. Progress feels natural, not exhausting. Suddenly, it's not "work" anymore — it's effortless and rewarding. Perhaps you'll even reach a flow state.

The Rule of Long-Term Goals

Months later, brimming with new skills, you hatch a plan to surprise your band buddies with a stellar performance and secure a spot in their lineup. The plan is simple: you'll gather them all together, ask for their favorite songs, and then perform them to perfection. They'll be so impressed that they'll immediately beg you to join their band.

You're already imagining it – the applause, the glory, the sheer joy of success.

It wasn't going to be.

Fast-forward to the day of your grand performance. It's a grand failure. You overestimated your ability to play songs you hadn't practiced. Your impromptu selections nosedived into a comedy of errors. Your friends are amused, but it's not the kind of amusement you'd hoped for.

What went wrong now?

You weren't in control. You underestimated the challenge and went in unprepared. You should have practiced their favorite songs ahead of time – ideally the exact songs they would request. If you'd rehearsed those tracks, you would have delivered a flawless performance. But instead, you winged it, hoping for talent, luck or God knows what else to save the day. It didn't.

These kinds of failures are a powerful source of discouragement. Countless people give up after failing to meet event-related goals. Nobody wants to experience failure repeatedly. You made a fool of yourself, and now you'd rather stay away from anything that reminds you of this disaster. Should you quit?

Not if you have a long-term goal.

The vision of playing in the band isn't just wishful thinking – it's a guiding light. Yes, you stumbled. But setbacks are just detours on the road to success. If you frame the botched performance as one small step in the larger journey, it suddenly doesn't feel so bad.

John Maynard Keynes was right when he said, "In the long run, we're all dead." But here's the catch: without long-term goals, we're often dead in the short run too.

***

How the Rules Work Together

This example beautifully illustrates the seamless integration of the first five rules, with an added boost from the rule of stupidity and the rule of meta-level. Each rule plays a vital role in increasing the likelihood of reaching your goal — like puzzle pieces that must fit together to complete the bigger picture.

The rule of curiosity acts as a filter, steering you away from unproductive paths and setting the stage for the other rules to work their magic. Without curiosity, the other rules lose much of their power. Curiosity is the entry point — it drives you to engage in meaningful pursuits.

Once you're on a path fueled by curiosity, you'll encounter obstacles. This is where the rule of talent comes in. It prevents you from falling into the "I'm not talented enough" trap. This rule propels you beyond the early struggles, which can feel like trudging through mud. Even with curiosity, most people quit the moment things get tough. The rule of talent ensures you don't.

Once you've conquered self-doubt, the rule of comfort zone comes into play. True efficiency happens only when you move past "grit mode" and into "effortless mode." The comfort zone isn't a trap; it's where you want to bring your new skills. You begin outside of it, but you should end up back inside — with new skills in tow. Mastery doesn't feel like effort; it feels like flow.

With efficiency comes the opportunity to prepare for specific milestones. This is where the rule of the Red Ferrari takes center stage. Event-related goals (like recitals, exams, or big meetings) require special attention. If you prepare like you're practicing for a red-carpet moment, you'll be ready when it matters most. The Ferrari isn't on the track every day — it shows up for the big races.

Even with all of these rules working together, setbacks are inevitable. Life isn't a smooth, linear path to success. This is where the rule of long-term goals becomes your safety net. Setbacks don't matter if you keep your eyes on the bigger picture. Without a long-term vision, a single failure can feel like the end of the road. With it, failures become mere potholes on the highway to success.

These rules collectively guide you through the entire lifespan of a goal – from the moment of inspiration to the moment of realization. They work as a filtering system, steadily weeding out distractions while amplifying the opportunities that matter. Each rule builds on the others, creating a comprehensive framework to combat biases, self-doubt, and motivational slumps. Together, they help you overcome the most common reasons for failure and stay on track.

While each rule can be helpful on its own, it's their combined effect that creates something truly powerful. These rules aren't isolated ideas; they're interlocking components of a system designed to outmaneuver doubt, self-sabotage, and mental shortcuts.

5 Rules, 5 Essential Questions to Ask Yourself

Whenever you feel like giving up on your goals, reflect on these five questions. Each one corresponds to one of the core rules, providing you with a diagnostic tool for pinpointing where things are going wrong.

1. **Am I truly curious about my goal?**
   If the answer is yes, it's worth continuing. If not, it might be a sign this goal isn't for you. Not every potential goal is worth pursuing. Stick to goals that spark genuine curiosity and interest. Passion fuels perseverance. Without it, you'll burn out.

2. **Do I believe I have the talent and intelligence to achieve this goal?**
   Believing that a lack of talent or intelligence is a barrier can become a self-fulfilling prophecy. You absolutely must banish those thoughts. If you believe you can learn and improve, you'll stay motivated. Doubt kills progress, but belief sparks it.

3. **Am I comfortable with the journey toward this goal?**
   At first, working toward a new goal may feel uncomfortable as you step outside your comfort zone. But if that discomfort persists for too long, motivation can wither. To succeed, the process must eventually feel natural — like it belongs in your daily routine. Your workflow should evolve into a comfortable, sustainable habit. If it doesn't, revisit the rule of comfort zone.

4. **Am I prepared enough?**
   Ask it before key events (like a tournament, exam, or presentation) where preparation is crucial. If you don't feel ready, put in more practice. The question should focus on specific, short-term events, not long-term progress.

5. **Do I have a long-term vision?**
   Short-term setbacks only hurt when you lack a long-term goal. If your goal is simply to win the next tournament, then losing feels catastrophic. But if your goal is to become a strong player, every loss is just another lesson. With a long-term vision, failures are no longer failures. They're just part of the process.

How to Succeed in the Workplace

The Rule of Stupidity

When considering a career change or starting out in a new position, it's easy to fall into the trap of believing that employees in those roles must be brainiacs with knowledge beyond your wildest dreams. This mindset makes the climb seem steeper than it is, crushing your motivation before you even start.

But this is where the rule of stupidity comes to the rescue. It reminds you that you don't need to be a genius to succeed in most jobs. In reality, most employees are not hyper-intelligent masterminds; they're regular people figuring things out as they go. Unless you're working with a once-in-a-generation prodigy, you only need a solid grasp of the basics to stay on pace with your colleagues.

This realization is liberating. It means you don't have to master everything on Day 1. You don't have to memorize the company's 200-page manual overnight or learn every advanced software tool in a week. You just need to focus on steady progress. Keep showing up, keep learning, and eventually, you'll get there.

Even if you do happen to work alongside a "superhuman" colleague – someone with mind-blowing knowledge or near-legendary skills – don't stress. The superhumans don't stay forever. By the time you've found your rhythm, they'll be long gone.

Instead of being paralyzed by fear, lean on the rule of stupidity. Remember, you don't need to be the smartest person in the room to succeed. Most of the time, you just need to be persistent, learn as you go, and stay in the game.

The Rule of Decision-Making

In your everyday office life, decision-making is an unavoidable part of the job. But at work, decisions aren't just abstract concepts – they shape your career. That's why sharpening your decision-making skills is essential for long-term success.

The rule of decision-making gives you a clear framework for approaching decisions at work. No more guesswork. No more knee-jerk reactions. Instead, you can make deliberate, strategic decisions. Here's a step-by-step process you can follow:

Clearly identify the problem at hand
It's impossible to make a good decision if you don't know what problem you're solving. Often, what we *think* is the problem isn't the actual problem. Take a step back, look at the big picture, and be honest about the real challenge you're facing.

Set a clear goal
The goal should be directly linked to solving the problem. Ask yourself, "What outcome would make this problem disappear?" This becomes your goal. If your problem is "we're missing deadlines," then your goal might be "deliver projects on time." If your problem is "we're losing customers," your goal could be "increase customer retention by 20%." Without a clear goal, your actions will lack direction.

Use backward induction
Start with the end goal and work backward, step-by-step, until you reach the present moment. Think about what needs to happen *just before* you achieve the goal, then what needs to happen before that, and so on. By tracing the logical steps backward, you'll create an actionable path forward. This process forces you to think critically and creates a step-by-step roadmap for achieving your goal.

If you apply this process consistently, it's guaranteed your decision-making skills will soon stand out in the office.

The Rule of Teamwork

When you're any good at what you do, people naturally start coming to you with their questions. But here's the thing: this doesn't happen randomly. People seek you out because they believe you'll have the answer.

You should believe it too.

You don't need to know everything, but you can always be helpful. If you know the answer, share it. If you don't, help them find it. Redirect them to the right person, suggest possible solutions, or offer to figure it out together. No one expects you to be a walking encyclopedia, but they'll respect you if you're a problem-solver.

This is how successful teams are built: not by people wearing the same uniform or working under the same logo, but by people helping each other when it counts. Every time you assist a teammate, you reinforce your value as a team player. Word spreads quickly. Before long, your boss notices. Then their boss notices. Soon, you're seen as one of the most valuable people in the department.

When you embrace the rule of teamwork, you'll see that helping others is a superpower in disguise. It makes you look more knowledgeable, more skilled, and more approachable. And here's the kicker: it's not even that hard to do.

Beyond Work: Succeeding in Life

The Rule of Agent Mulder

Sometimes, the decisions that shape your day aren't your own. Instructions, proposals, and demands from others — especially from bosses — can dictate your path. But just because someone tells you what to do doesn't mean it's the right move. That's where the rule of Agent Mulder comes into play.

Question everything.

If your boss gives you instructions, don't just nod along like a robot. Take a moment to assess the logic behind the request.

Does it make sense? If it does, proceed with confidence. But if you spot inconsistencies, flaws, or outright nonsense, that's your cue to speak up. Voice your concerns and propose adjustments.

Why waste your time and energy on something that shouldn't be done in the first place? If you can reason with your boss and get them to see the flaws, great. But if your boss is one of those "I'm always right" types who can't be swayed by logic, don't fight a losing battle. Do the task as instructed, get it done, and move on. Not every hill is worth dying on.

But don't let it end there. After the task is complete, take a step back and reflect. Go to the meta level and ask yourself if you're in the right place with the right people. If your boss consistently prioritizes bad decisions and ignores logic, maybe it's time to reconsider your working environment. Life's too short to waste it under the command of clowns.

The Rule of Meta-level

Occasionally, step back from your life and look at it from a distance. From this elevated perspective, you can see patterns, flaws, and blind spots that are invisible when you're stuck in the day-to-day grind.

Ask yourself questions like:

- What areas of my life need to change?
- Am I playing my roles as well as I could be? (Parent, partner, friend, employee, leader – these are all roles.)

Chances are, you're underperforming in at least one of these roles or there is something very wrong in your life, but you just haven't realized it yet. And that's not a criticism. It's a fact of human nature. We all have blind spots.

But when you activate the rule of meta-level, you reveal your true colors. You see yourself the way others see you. And while it's not always a flattering view, it's an honest one. From here, you can make adjustments, break bad habits, and upgrade your primary self.

This concept isn't just for personal growth. It applies to work, relationships, and every aspect of life. You can use it to realize that your true curiosity lies in playing the violin, or to recognize that it's time to escape your clown bosses once and for all. When you zoom out, you gain clarity. When you gain clarity, you make smarter choices. And smarter choices lead to better outcomes.

Don't just live your life. See it from above. Then improve it.

***

Final Thoughts

You've done it. You now hold all the pieces of the success puzzle and understand how they interconnect. Each piece represents a simple rule, but together, they form a powerful framework that can guide you through the ocean of failures toward the island of success.

Every rule on its own has the potential to push you forward. But when combined, their impact becomes far greater than the sum of their parts. This synergy is where the magic happens.

How can following ten simple rules make the difference between failure and success? The answer lies in the core of our struggles. Often, we convince ourselves that success is a distant peak, too steep to climb and not worth the effort. This belief is rooted in our evolutionary past, where conserving energy and avoiding unnecessary risks increased our chances of survival. But in modern life, this instinct works against us. It drains our motivation, leads to subpar performance, and keeps us stuck in the cycle of mediocrity.

The worst part? This cycle feeds itself. Self-doubt leads to inaction, inaction leads to failure, and failure reinforces the belief that success is out of reach. It becomes a self-fulfilling prophecy.

The good news? You can break the cycle.

While we can't change our natural inclination toward doubt and laziness, we can train our minds to act as though those tendencies don't exist. That's the purpose of the ten rules in this book. They were designed to strip away the most common reasons for failure and replace them with a framework for sustained progress. That's why they work.

Success doesn't have to be as extreme as Lady Astor and Sir Winston Churchill made it seem in their legendary exchange of insults. You don't need to poison your husband just because he's Winston Churchill, nor do you need to kill yourself just because your wife is Lady Astor.

Instead, success comes from taking a much simpler, calmer approach: find the root causes of failure, neutralize them, and stay the course. The path to your goals is not as difficult as most people think.

After facing my share of failures before eventually finding success, I can personally vouch for the transformative power of these ten rules. I'm living proof that they work. There's nothing special about me (aside from being tone-deaf), which means there's every reason to believe they'll work for you too.

Success is not reserved for a privileged few. It's not about being born with brilliance, talent, or luck. It's about using the right tools and following the right rules.

Now that you have those pieces in hand, let them work their magic. Use them to unlock your potential and piece together your own success puzzle.

Epilogue: Every Hand Can Be a Winner and Every Hand Can Be a Loser

Each player must accept the cards life deals him or her;
but once they are in hand, he or she must alone decide
how to play the cards in order to win the game.

Voltaire

Outsmarted by the Divine

A man climbed to the top of a hill to talk to God. He asked, "God, what is a million years to you?"

God answered, "A minute."

The man then asked, "But God, how much is a million dollars to you?"

"A penny," replied God.

The man then cleverly said, "God, could you give me a penny?"

"Sure," replied God, "Wait a minute."

***

The Game of Life Is Winnable

You take your seat at a poker table, ready to test your skills in a game of Texas Hold'em. The dealer slides you the Ace of Hearts and Ace of Spades – the best possible starting hand. It's a dream start. Your strategy is clear: if your opponents play passively, you take the lead; if they get aggressive, you re-raise them into oblivion. Your goal is to maximize value from your premium hand.

But poker doesn't care about your plans.

The flop comes: Seven of Clubs, Eight of Clubs, Nine of Clubs. Suddenly, your Aces lose their shine. You still have the strongest pair, but now your opponents could easily have a straight or a flush. You bet to protect your hand, but when faced with a raise and a re-raise, it's time to muck your Aces with the speed of light. What started as a monster hand now looks like a slow trainwreck, and it should be played as such.

Now, imagine you're dealt a less glamorous hand: Six of Clubs and Ten of Clubs. Pre-flop, it's a hand nobody writes home about — mediocre at best. You need special conditions just to see the flop. But then comes the same flop: Seven of Clubs, Eight of Clubs, Nine of Clubs. This time, it's a miracle. You've just hit a straight flush — one of the rarest and most powerful hands in poker. Suddenly, you're in control. You bet, you raise, you trap, and you milk every chip from your opponents.

The lesson is clear: starting hands matter, but how you play them matters more. No hand is strong in every flop, but for every hand there exist flops where they can succeed. You don't control the flop, but you control when your money goes in.

Life works the same way.

Each of us is dealt a unique hand, but our future is not determined by the cards we're dealt — it's determined by how we play them. As Kenny Rogers sang in the poker classic "The Gambler," every hand is a winner and every hand is a loser, meaning that everyone has the potential for both success and failure. Our fate isn't sealed by our starting hand. It's shaped by the decisions we make, the risks we take, and how well we play the game of life.

With the ten rules you now have at your disposal, you possess the tools to play the game of life well. These rules are universal. They're not just for the "naturally gifted" or "special" people. Even the most sluggish, unmotivated person can use these principles to succeed — I can say this with confidence because they worked for me.

I hope this book helps you play the game of life better. I hope it shows you that success isn't something reserved for "other people" or "the lucky few." Success is within your reach. It's about overcoming the natural tendencies that hold you back, mastering the clever tricks that lead to big results, and making the most of the cards you're dealt.

Above all, I hope you found this book to be a rewarding read.

Words to Remember

Before you go, I want to leave you with a collection of memorable phrases and idioms from this book. Think of them as your "pocket phrases" — little reminders to help you stay on track. Some of them are original concepts introduced here for the first time. Even if you think the entire book is nonsense (as pointless as my PhD thesis or that self-help book your aunt gave you last Christmas), you might still impress your friends by dropping a few of these phrases into conversation.

Here they are:

- Every master was once a beginner.
- Curiosity killed the cat ... but saved the catkind.
- Without curiosity, you build houses. With curiosity, you build homes.
- Talent isn't a "real thing" — it's a story we tell ourselves to justify failure.
- Talent is one of the biggest and most dangerous lies ever told.
- When you're in flow, you're not chasing success. Success is chasing you.
- The better you get at something, the more fun it becomes.
- You don't fail your way to success. You learn your way to success.
- Nobody hates routines. People hate boring routines. Nobody hates the routine of cashing a paycheck.
- One can never truly excel while being okay with failing.
- In the long run, we are all dead, but we still need long-term goals to survive the short run.
- It's impossible to predict the future, but it doesn't mean we should live as if there is none.

- Don't borrow from tomorrow.
- The idea that people are highly knowledgeable in their specialties is often an illusion. Everybody is stupid in almost everything.
- The biggest mistake people make isn't being clueless. It's assuming that everyone else has a clue.
- If something doesn't make sense, ask — you'll often find that nobody else understands it either.
- A 5 out of 100 feels like a genius next to a 0.
- There is no greater waste than spending time and resources on something that should not be done at all.
- If you've identified the wrong problem, you'll chase the wrong goal.
- It's not very hard to make correct decisions; it's correct to make hard decisions.
- When asked a question, assume you are the best person to answer.
- Five disconnected stars don't make a constellation. They just burn out.
- If you never stop the act, it stops being an act. (You're not pretending to be a better person anymore — you *are* a better person).
- We are all lying to ourselves. If you think you don't, you're lying to yourself.
- We are far more willing to recognize the need for change in other people's lives than in our own.
- If you think you're the smartest person in the room, you stop listening, stop questioning, and stop learning.
- Success is not reserved for a privileged few.
- While we can't change our natural inclination toward doubt and laziness, we can train our minds to act as though those tendencies don't exist.

***

You may have noticed that every chapter in this book begins with a captivating story and ends with a reflection on its relevance to the topic.

So, naturally, you might be wondering what a man trying to swindle a penny from God has to do with the concept of "playing your hand in life."

Honestly, nothing at all. But it's a humorous tale worth sharing.

Business Books

Recent Bestsellers from Business Books Are:

From 50 to 500

Jonathan Dapra, Richard Dapra and Jonas Akerman

An engaging and innovative small business leadership framework guaranteed to strengthen a leader's effectiveness to drive company growth and results.

Paperback: 978-1-78904-743-1 ebook: 978-1-78904-744-8

Be Visionary

Marty Strong

Be Visionary: Strategic Leadership in the Age of Optimization

Demonstrates to existing and aspiring leaders the positive impact of applying visionary creativity and decisiveness to achieve spectacular long-range results while balancing the day-to-day.

Paperback: 978-1-78535-432-8 ebook: 978-1-78535-433-5

Finding Sustainability

Trent A. Romer

Journey to eight states, three national parks and three countries to experience the life-changing education that led Trent A. Romer to find sustainability for his plastic-bag manufacturing business and himself.

Paperback: 978-1-78904-601-4 ebook: 978-1-78904-602-1

Inner Brilliance, Outer Shine

Estelle Read

Optimise your success, performance, productivity and well-being to lead your best business life.

Paperback: 978-1-78904-803-2 ebook: 978-1-78904-804-9

Tomorrow's Jobs Today

Rafael Moscatel and Abby Jane Moscatel

Discover leadership secrets and technology strategies being pioneered by today's most innovative business executives and renowned brands across the globe.

Paperback: 978-1-78904-561-1 ebook: 978-1-78904-562-8

Secrets to Successful Property Investment

Deb Durbin

Your complete guide to building a property portfolio.

Paperback: 978-1-78904-818-6 ebook: 978-1-78904-819-3

The Effective Presenter

Ryan Warriner

The playbook to professional presentation success!

Paperback: 978-1-78904-795-0 ebook: 978-1-78904-796-7

The Beginner's Guide to Managing

Mikil Taylor

A how-to guide for first-time managers adjusting to their new leadership roles.

Paperback: 978-1-78904-583-3 ebook: 978-1-78904-584-0

Forward

Elizabeth Moran

A practical playbook for leaders to guide their teams through their organization's next big change.

Paperback: 978-1-78279-289-5 ebook: 978-1-78279-291-8

Readers of ebooks can buy or view any of these bestsellers by clicking on the live link in the title. Most titles are published in paperback and as an ebook. Paperbacks are available in traditional bookshops. Both print and ebook formats are available online.

Find more titles and sign up to our readers' newsletter at www.collectiveinkbooks.com/business-books